T0313731

Strictly for Volunteers

111 Tips, Ideas and Morsels of Wisdom for Anyone Who Volunteers

Scott C. Stevenson, Editor

WILEY

For general information on our other products and services or for technical support, please contact our Customer Care Department within the United States at (800) 762-2974, outside the United States at (317) 572-3993 or fax (317) 572-4002.

Wiley publishes in a variety of print and electronic formats and by print-on-demand. Some material included with standard print versions of this book may not be included in e-books or in print-on-demand. If this book refers to media such as a CD or DVD that is not included in the version you purchased, you may download this material at http://booksupport.wiley.com. For more information about Wiley products, visit www.wiley.com.

978-1-118-69319-3   ISBN

978-1-118-70408-0   ISBN (online)

Strictly for Volunteers

111 Tips, Ideas & Morsels of Wisdom for Anyone Who Volunteers

Published by

Stevenson, Inc.

P.O. Box 4528 • Sioux City, Iowa • 51104
Phone 712.239.3010 • Fax 712.239.2166
www.stevensoninc.com

Strictly for Volunteers

111 Tips, Ideas & Morsels of Wisdom for Anyone Who Volunteers

Strictly for Volunteers

111 Tips, Ideas & Morsels of Wisdom for Anyone Who Volunteers

1. Use Your Hobbies to Further Your Cause

Make use of your interests to increase your enthusiasm for volunteering.

Do you have any hobbies? What are they? Could they somehow be used to help the organization for which you volunteer? That may sound unlikely at first, but you may be surprised by how a hobby could be used to further a cause.

Here's a small sampling of hobbies that have helped volunteer-driven agencies:

- A quilter who donated a quilt as a raffle item and generated more than $1,000 for her agency.

- A baseball card collector who organized a baseball card show with a percentage of entry fees going to the hospital where he volunteers.

- An amateur photographer who derived pleasure from taking shots of volunteers for feature stories.

- An individual who loved restoring furniture and used her talent to refurbish two hospital lounges.

2. Three Tips for Avoiding Procrastination

Time management tip: We all deal with procrastination, but there are techniques you can use to overcome it.

Putting off a task not only causes problems for you but may have other negative consequences of which you're not even aware. Be an example to fellow volunteers by completing tasks before their deadlines. To overcome procrastination:

1. **Accept that it doesn't have to be perfect.** An adequate job done on time is better than an "excellent but late" completion.

2. **Break up the job into more manageable (less overwhelming) parts**, then go for "the five-minute plan." Tell yourself you'll just work at one part of the project for five minutes. You'll be surprised by how easy it is to keep going once you simply get started.

3. **Reward yourself.** If the job doesn't include any sort of reward for having completed it on time, come up with your own reward as a self motivator.

3. Evaluate Your Volunteer Time

Whether you volunteer for one, two or more deserving causes, do you ever take the time to evaluate how you're spending those hours? What percentage of the time are you in meetings? How much time do you spend working at a project as opposed to down time that may include waiting on someone, travel time to and from your volunteer destination and more?

Keep a time log, such as the example shown here, for a period of one or two months. List dates, hours, location and what you did during that period of time. Then, at the end of one or two months, evaluate how your total volunteer time was used. Although there may be no surprises, in some instances volunteers will make adjustments in the use of their limited time. They may decide to spend more time on particular projects, focus their efforts more with one organization or make any number of changes.

See if a time log helps you create a more rewarding volunteer experience and a greater volunteer contribution.

Volunteer Time Log			
Date	Hours	Location	Use of Volunteer Time

4. Help Recruit, Train Others Before Moving On

Does this sound familiar? You've enjoyed a lasting relationship with a particular nonprofit organization, but you're beginning to realize that you can't go on volunteering forever. If so, how do you make sure all your years of work don't just unravel once you leave?

Advice for the vet

To preserve and foster your legacy, consider spending your remaining time as a volunteer recruiting and training others who will one day help assume responsibility for some of what you and your fellow volunteers have accomplished to date.

Come up with a plan — in conjunction with appropriate staff — to handpick the right volunteers to assume "apprentice" roles while you're still actively involved. If it's unrealistic to assume one volunteer could fulfill all of what you've done over time, break the job down and recruit two or three volunteers who have the time to take on a part of what you have done. Recognizing that not all volunteers may be in it for the long run, you may even want to recruit pairs of volunteers to share jobs, knowing it's possible some attrition may occur.

What you can do now, before stepping out of your active role, will help ensure a smooth transition down the road.

> **Know Your Mission**
>
> Most charitable organizations have a mission statement that serves as the foundation of all their work. As a volunteer, take time to become familiar with and support that mission.

5. Request a Letter of Reference From Your Volunteer Supervisor

Applying for a job or graduate school? Need a letter of reference from your volunteer manager or supervisor? Keep these tips in mind when requesting a reference letter:

Don't overlook your volunteer experiences when applying for graduate school or a new job.

1. Always ask first. Don't include someone as a reference without getting his or her permission first.

2. Don't ask "Could you write a letter of reference for me?" Rather, ask "Do you think you know me well enough to be able to write a positive letter of reference for me?"

3. Provide your referee with the following information:
   - The purpose of the letter of reference (e.g., job application, application for graduate school, scholarship, etc.).
   - The names, titles and addresses of the persons to whom the letter should be sent (including stamps) or specific information as to how the letter will be delivered to the recipients (e.g., in a sealed envelope that you will pick up, etc.).
   - The date the letter must be received.
   - Forms to be completed by the referee.
   - A copy of your current resume or summary of experience, including community/volunteer service.
   - A statement of your professional/career goals.
   - Where you can be reached in case of questions (e-mail, phone and address).

4. Give the person at least 10 days to two weeks time to write the letter. Don't be afraid to follow up on it.

5. After the letter has been sent, be sure to thank the referee.

> **Volunteers and Tax Deductions**
>
> Did you know your out-of-pocket expenses when you volunteer could be tax-deductible? IRS form 526 outlines: which organizations qualify, what you can deduct and what you can't, when to deduct, limits to deductions and how to keep records. Check out www.irs.gov/publications/p526/index.html

6.

Volunteer Liability

Did you know that you could be sued individually for injuries you cause while acting in a volunteer capacity? What is your organization doing to protect you from such situations?

Tip for Volunteer Groups

Select one person to serve as your group's primary contact. This person will receive all communications on behalf of the group regarding volunteering, and will be responsible for communicating with all group members.

Support Fellow Volunteers In Multiple Ways

To help fellow volunteers become all that they can be, it's important that you give them your full support. To do that:

✓ Offer to take them to or from volunteer jobs.

✓ Never hesitate to tell them they're doing a great job.

✓ Help be a calming influence during times of conflict.

✓ Step in an lend a hand now and then.

✓ Introduce them to other volunteers and paid staff.

Identify What Motivates You Most

Part of being an accomplished volunteer is knowing what energizes you most. If you're turned on by a particular task or situation, you'll do a far better job and want to come back for more. It's as simple as that.

To help identify what most invigorates you about your work as a volunteer or board member, take a minute and complete the following interest inventory. By prioritizing your top interests, you can make better future choices when it comes to projects and tasks.

ENTHUSIASM INDEX

When you look back on your past volunteer experiences, what energized you most? Review the following items, assigning a 1, 2 or 3 to each.

Rate Yourself
1 = Really enjoy
2 = Willing to do
3 = Little or no satisfaction

_____ Working in a group setting
_____ Meeting new people
_____ Working with people I know
_____ Working alone
_____ Assuming leadership for a project
_____ Taking orders and doing my assigned task
_____ Working outside
_____ Working inside
_____ Doing routine tasks
_____ Having a variety of assignments
_____ Working for a short period of time
_____ Helping others
_____ Using my professional expertise
_____ Doing something unrelated to my profession
_____ Working scheduled hours
_____ Working on my own time schedule
_____ Meeting the public
_____ Working behind the scenes
_____ Using my hands
_____ Using my brain
_____ Instructing others
_____ Working on projects that directly impact the agency
_____ Doing detail work
_____ Helping with larger, long-term projects

7. Take Full Responsibility for Assignments

If for some you can't complete a volunteer assignment you agreed to, don't simply notify the office and force staff to find alternatives. Take responsibility for finding a replacement and ensuring that your work gets done:

Be accountable for yourself

1. Find a competent replacement.
2. Know that your replacement knows exactly what is expected of him/her.
3. Notify the office of your actions.
4. Follow up with your replacement to confirm completion of work.

8. Label Yourself Community Volunteer. Go Ahead — You're Special!

We've all attended meetings in which we're asked to introduce ourselves and state our title or occupation. While many state their professional positions, there are always a small handful of individuals who simply refer to themselves as "community volunteer." If you happen to fall into that category — people who may not have a "paying" job but are active in a number of community organizations — you're special. You're special not only because of your extraordinary selflessness but also because you have the distinct perspective of seeing and learning how a number of nonprofit organizations and agencies operate. Because of your continued exposure to a number of organizations, you're privy to the various ways in which meetings are run, the manner in which projects and programs are implemented and much more.

Volunteers 'in the know'

In your capacity as "community volunteer," you can use your vantage point to share improved ways of doing any number of things. First, recognize the unique position you hold. Then don't be afraid to share your experiences and observations with staff and other volunteers whenever you come across a better way of planning, organizing, developing policies or whatever the issue might be. Whether or not they vocalize the fact, others respect those who make a full-time job as "community volunteer" and are ready and willing to listen to your suggestions. You possess a wealth of information and know-how, so don't be shy about offering your insight.

9. Avoid Putting Off What Should be Completed Now

The monthly meeting's over and you've just been assigned new tasks due by next month's meeting. If you're like many volunteers, you'll wait until three weeks from now (or later) before you start, only to realize too late that you should have begun sooner.

Meeting deadlines

To avoid missing project deadlines, try these time management practices:

1. **Begin at least part of the assignment the very day you learn about it.** Often, simply beginning a project helps to overcome the barrier of avoiding it and get the ball rolling.

2. **If you're unsure about how to do any aspect of the assignment, talk to someone who's done it before.** It's easy to procrastinate over something that seems even somewhat unclear.

3. **Try a little self indulgence:** If you get the project completed within two weeks, reward yourself modestly. If you complete it within 72 hours, make it an extra-special reward.

10. Keep a List of Questions That Need Answers

Become the best that you can be.

Becoming the best possible volunteer means becoming more proficient at your job and more knowledgable about the agency for which you work. To help in that effort, get in the habit of jotting down questions whenever they arise — questions about what you do, how it was done before, how it impacts those served by the agency and more.

QUESTIONS THAT NEED ANSWERS	
<u>DATE</u>	<u>QUESTION</u>
September 2	How many patients does this hospital serve (on average) throughout the course of a year?
September 6	How much time would it take to be trained to work in the gift shop (in addition to what I'm doing now)?
September 12	If I see something going on that appears suspicious, to whom should I report that information?
September 12	If weather prevents me from driving, does the hospital have pick up/delivery service? How does that work?

Also, don't hesitate to ask questions that go beyond your immediate job responsibilities. The more you know, the better volunteer you will be.

Maintain a "questions that need answers" note pad. Then, whenever a question about anything pops up, write it down. Wait until you have several questions that need answers before sitting down with the appropriate staff person to get them answered. Then, when you do meet, jot down the answers for future reference.

11. Displace Negative Thoughts With Positive Ones

The power of positive thinking.

Remember what you learned in physics class: two objects can't occupy the same space at the same time (e.g., when you put a brick in a liquid, the liquid gets displaced). Well, your thoughts are objects, too. Therefore, two thoughts can't occupy the same space at the same time. You can't think of failure and success at the same time. It's impossible. So if you stop concentrating on failure and start focusing on success, the "success brick" will displace the "failure liquid."

12. Learn to Deal With Those Who Complain

Work at improving your coping skills.

When you hear a complaint from a fellow volunteer, listen calmly and paraphrase. Rephrasing the complaint forces the individual to define the problem. Avoid being sympathetic to a nonstop complainer; it only reinforces negative behavior. Instead, ask the complainer to document each complaint and list possible solutions.

13. Rate Your Ability to be a Team Player

A cooperative spirit among volunteers makes the task at hand much more fun and fulfilling.

How do you rate as a team player among your volunteer peers? Are you complimentary of others' contributions? Are you pulling your share (or more) of the load?

Sometimes lack of group cooperativeness can be the biggest detriment to success. Likewise, a group whose members work in concert with one another becomes energized with nothing to hold it back. Everyone supports one another and goes the extra mile to carry his/her fair share.

Complete the simple exercise at left to help you measure your team player strengths and weaknesses. Its purpose is to help you identify behaviors that lend themselves to — or detract from — working as a team.

Knowing where you stand — and where you could possibly improve — will help make you an exemplary team player in future endeavors.

14. How to Deal With a Micromanager

Job satisfaction

Working with a micromanager — someone who peers over your shoulder while you work, worries every detail to death or insists you do everything his/her way — can be frustrating and stressful. But what can you do? You're not likely to change the person. What you *can* change is the way you respond to the situation.

Here are some ways to cope with a micromanager:

- *Remember everyone feels the pain.* Micromanaging hurts people, but micromanagers are in pain, too. They take on the burdens of micromanagement in a futile attempt to stop the pain.

- *The problem is never the problem — the coping is the problem.* Since micromanagement is a way of asserting control, try to understand what your supervisor sees as out of control.

- *Focus on the things you like about your work.* Celebrating the tasks you enjoy creates energy for dealing with the more difficult aspects of your work.

- *Keep your options open.* You can always choose to leave. That choice might not be appealing, but you can choose it, nonetheless. If you stay, stay because staying is the best option available.

> ### Not Motivated To Exercise?
>
> Not feeling motivated to exercise? Enlist the help of others. Create a friendly competition with your fellow volunteers. For example, the team whose members exercise for 30 minutes, three times a week for three months wins a prize. You decide what the prize is (make it a healthy one!).

15. Act as a Resource in Lining Up Talks

Educate the public

If the organization you volunteer for offers presentations to groups and civic organizations, do your part to help connect the agency with groups that would welcome a program.

Consider each of the civic groups and organizations to which you belong. Find out who is in charge of scheduling programs and how you can serve as a catalyst in getting a speaking engagement set up. Provide the appropriate agency rep in charge of giving presentations with useful background information about the group to which he/she will be speaking (e.g., number of members, location, possible dates for a presentation, etc.).

16. Five Actions You Can Take to Enlist More Volunteers

Here are five ways you can encourage others to become volunteers like you:

1. **Talk up your volunteer experiences at work.** Extend an invitation in your company's internal newsletter, if appropriate.

2. **Don't overlook family and close friends.** You may love volunteering together!

3. **Say a good word at public appearances.** When you have an opportunity to address a group during a speech, presentation or gathering, work in a positive comment about the organization for which you volunteer.

4. **Spread the word in clubs and organizations to which you belong, including your church/synagogue.** You may convince your club to take on a project.

5. **Extend an open invitation in writing or by e-mail.** Do so in the body of a letter or as a postscript: "P.S. Did you know I've volunteered with the Ames Literacy Guild for five years? I love it, and would love if you'd join me! Call me so we can talk."

> ### Avoid Knee-jerk E-mail Reply
>
> E-mail's greatest benefit can also be its greatest drawback. When you sit down to do e-mail, your mindset is typically to get through it as quickly as possible. However, this approach can generate knee-jerk reactions to others' questions, solicitations of opinions, requests and recommendations. Speed can be a potentially negative habit, so take the time to write a reasoned response.

17. Lost Art of Storytelling Finds Welcome Reception in Pittsburgh

Volunteer-driven events worth your consideration.

Some may think it a dying art, but storytelling is alive and well in Pittsburgh, thanks to the Three Rivers Storytelling Festival sponsored by Northland Public Library and Foundation.

Every August, more than 1,000 people attend the two-day festival, featuring two storytelling stages, workshops, a storytelling store and world-class talent. The event grosses about $10,000 a year to help supplement the library's collection.

The festival started in 2000, says Pat McCarthy, manager of volunteer services. "We were looking for a unique fundraiser with a direct correlation to reading," says McCarthy, "and storytelling seemed like a natural fit."

The event starts Friday with a series of fee-based workshops provided by the resident storytellers. Evening concerts on Friday and Saturday bring together all of the featured storytellers, so they can feed off one another's creativity and enthusiasm while spinning their tales. Throughout the day on Saturday, both featured and local talents have the stage to themselves at various intervals.

While the storytellers receive a nominal fee, most costs are covered through grants. In-kind donations of food and beverages are also provided by area businesses.

More than 150 volunteers are recruited to assist with setup/cleanup, ticket sales, children's activities, etc. Each national storyteller is assigned a volunteer "angel" who transports the storyteller to and from the airport or hotel and assists the storyteller throughout the event.

If your organization would like to sponsor a storytelling festival, start small — you can always expand later, says McCarthy. "At first, we weren't sure if it would work in our community," she says. "It's taken a lot of education on our part, because people tend to associate storytelling strictly with children. But it's fun for all ages."

Advance tickets to the festival are $9 for adults and $4.50 for children. Admission at the door is $10 for adults and $5 for children. Children under six are admitted free of charge. The fee to attend one of the workshops is $35.

Source: Pat McCarthy, Manager, Volunteer Services, Northland Public Library, Pittsburgh, PA. Phone (412) 366-8100. Email: mccarthyp@einetwork.net

---

Meeting Organizers Who Show Up Late

Although annoying, most meetings can start on time even if some participants habitually arrive late. But what do you do if the chronic latecomer is the meeting organizer?

If the person who calls the meeting is always late, pose this gentle but noticeable question: "Would it be more convenient to start next week's meeting 15 minutes later?"

---

18. Volunteering Can Be a Career Booster

Your volunteer experiences can actually help to strengthen certain career skills.

Volunteering not only brings great benefit to the community, it can also give your career a boost.

Serving as a board member can help you develop valuable leadership skills: creativity, negotiation, collaboration, problem-solving, persuasion, etc.

Volunteering in a leadership capacity shows hiring managers you have character and initiative and can give you an edge in the hiring process.

It also raises your visibility and broadens your network, which can be extremely helpful down the road.

19. Meeting Leaders Should Facilitate, Not Monopolize

Exemplary leadership skills

If you have the honor of leading a meeting, be mindful of your role: A good leader should not monopolize meetings, but rather serve as a facilitator who encourages others to participate as fully as possible.

Your role as a catalyst should be to encourage others to offer input and ideas. And when they do, affirm them, even if you might disagree with their opinion or suggestion: "While that solution might have some key challenges associated with it, it's certainly worth our consideration."

20. Adjusting to a New Volunteer Manager

Adjusting to a new job can be difficult, even when you're the boss (or in this case, the volunteer manager).

When you're new, you're being analyzed by a lot of people. They're evaluating how you work, how much commitment you have to the new place and people, your sincerity and your abilities to pick things up fast.

Whether you're the newcomer or your volunteer manager is, it's up to you to make — and sustain — a great first impression. Here are some tips for making the best of your relationship with the new "boss:"

Do your part to forge a positive relationship with paid staff.

1. **Get a clear picture of your manager's expectations** — What exactly does your manager expect from you? The best way to find out is to ask.

2. **Communicate what you need to do your job well** — Because your manager is new to the organization, he or she may not be aware of your strengths and abilities, so it is important that you make that information available.

3. **Go out of your way to solve problems** — As a rule, you should always strive to seek solutions to problems rather than just push them off onto your manager's desk.

The changes that a new manager brings in can be very positive for your organization. Look at those changes as opportunities and challenges, and you'll find that working with a new manager is far easier than you anticipated.

21. Confirm Other Volunteers' Assignments in Writing

When you're in charge of a committee that meets periodically and requires action on the part of committee members between each meeting, it's wise to send a memo (or e-mail) that confirms what's expected of each individual and by when. A written communication that spells out individual duties accomplishes three important goals:

1. It places greater accountability on the volunteer who agreed to complete particular tasks by a certain date.

2. It shows the volunteer that you, as committee chair, are aware of what's expected of him/her.

3. It leaves no room for confusion about what's to be done.

At right is an example of a committee meeting follow-up memo confirming the assignment of one committee member:

MEMO   HARTLEY *FOOD BANK*

To: Marie Currans, Recruitment Committee Member
From: Jane Saunders, Chair, Recruitment Committee
RE: Volunteer Enlistment
Date: January 11, 2007

This is to serve as a confirmation (from our January 10 meeting) that you agreed to meet with the following individuals to determine their willingness to participate in our day-long food collection effort.

It's important that we know by January 22 who will be a part of this project. Please call me with your results or e-mail me at jsaunders@aol.com on or before that date.

Thanks and good luck!

Potential Volunteer	Daytime Phone	Evening Phone
Susan Eberheart	390-3345	371-2187
Michelle Sievers	393-4744	371-3220
Tom Burkfechtel	353-2295	343-2264
Marty Toth	390-6430	371-4475
Dave Behrens	393-6354	376-1131
Harry Cartwright	393-7740	376-0505
Patrice Merryweather	390-5222	371-3499
Melony Horst	353-2290	343-4446

22. Don't Leave a Meeting Without...

You don't have to be in charge of a meeting to play a positive role in it. Contribute by following through on these suggestions.

✓ Stepping forward and agreeing to help in some way.

✓ Having your "to do" list down on paper, with deadlines.

✓ Having general consensus on what matters most.

✓ Putting aside controversial issues and concluding on a positive note.

✓ Having some sense of what should be on the next meeting's agenda.

✓ Thanking the meeting chair for his/her leadership.

23. Assign Someone 'Timekeeper' Duties

Meetings management tip

Here's a tip to make your meetings run more smoothly: Designate a timekeeper. It's the timekeeper's responsibility to keep the meeting within the previously set time frame.

Reward the timekeeper with a special (inexpensive) treat — a handwritten thank-you, an e-card or a piece of candy.

Source: Donna Stutler, Volunteer Services Coordinator, Damar Services, Inc., Camby, IN. Email: donnas@damar.org

24. Why Having a Goal Isn't Enough

Goal-setting procedures

It isn't enough to simply *have* goals. You also need to know *why* you want to achieve them. Without a strong and persuasive reason behind each of your goals, you'll never get what you want.

Try this exercise: Take one of your goals and answer the following questions with as much detail and emotion as possible:

✓ What will achieving your goal do for you physically? Mentally? Emotionally? Financially? Spiritually?

✓ What will you think of yourself years from now if you achieve your goal?

✓ What will failing to achieve your goal cost you physically? Mentally? Emotionally? Financially? Spiritually?

✓ How will failing to achieve your goal negatively affect your friends and family? What will it cost them in the long run?

✓ What will you think of yourself years from now if you never achieve your goal?

25. Consider Spending Your Family Vacation Volunteering

Family volunteering idea

Family vacations provide wonderful memories. Why not choose a vacation where everyone in the family can volunteer together?

Nonprofit organizations across the country offer volunteering opportunities that range from overseas trips to ongoing events. For example, you can volunteer for a week in places like Nepal, Africa and South America with the Global Citizens Network (www.globalcitizens.org). This group offers packages that include everything but airfare. Plus, the costs are tax deductible.

Other groups, like the Sierra Club (www.sierraclub.org), offer family vacation packages across the United States, including Cape Cod.

Or, you can go another route. If you already have a planned vacation spot, check out Habitat for Humanity (www.habitat.org), to see if they're building a house in that area. Contact the local office directly; they're always looking for helpers.

26. Put Your Volunteer Director in Touch With Would-be Volunteers

Here's a great way to help your volunteer services director network with more people and put her/his recruiting talents to work. Purchase a complimentary membership to some organization for her/him — the Chamber of Commerce, a civic group or, if appropriate, a country club.

Do your part to help your volunteer services director network and spread the word about volunteer opportunities.

Many volunteer budgets are too limited to allow memberships in such organizations. Your thoughtful gesture would allow the volunteer director to become more visible and better able to recruit volunteers from a particular segment of your community.

Give it some thought.

27. If it's Your Job, Learn to Take Better Minutes

How can I take better minutes during our meetings?

"I used to take minutes with a paper and pencil, but found it too frustrating to capture all of the information needed. Now I bring a laptop with me and try to type in the main points of conversation. I keep an agenda of the meeting and type in the agenda heading before I type in the information, just to remind myself what the conversation is referring to. After the meeting, I condense the minutes and take out whatever is not needed or not clear."

> — *Laura Philbert, Assistant to the CEO,*
> *Shelter for Abused Women & Children, Naples, FL*

"Ask the president for an agenda. Create a template with major points, leaving space to take notes (e.g., heading with date, attendees and absentees, president's report, treasurer's report, committee reports — list each, new business and old business)."

> — *Bonnie L. Olson, Executive Director,*
> *Komen Southwest Florida Affiliate, Bonita Springs, FL*

More Tips On Taking Minutes

More tips for taking effective minutes from Robert's Rules of Order, Newly Revised:

1. Record what's done, not said.
2. Use wide margins for corrections.
3. Send the board president an advance copy.
4. You needn't mention seconds on motions.
5. Separate subjects with paragraphs.

28. Make a Point to Document All First-time Projects

If you're in charge of (or taking part in) a first-time project, help future volunteers avoid having to recreate the wheel by documenting every step you take. In fact, encourage everyone involved to take notes and submit them to you at the end of the project. These valuable notes will save future volunteers time and maybe even money if you make a point to document all procedures along the way.

Passing the baton to other volunteers

Project notes should answer these basic questions:

✓ What was the project's purpose?

✓ How many volunteers were involved and what were their responsibilities?

✓ How was the project broken into manageable "pieces?" Who did what?

✓ What was the project's timeline from start to finish?

✓ What funds were needed for what and where did you get them?

✓ What went wrong with the project? What went right?

✓ What changes would you make in the future? What would you do differently?

29. One Instance in Which Gossip is Good

Actions that distinguish leaders

When delivering information to staff or fellow volunteers, it's important to factor in their emotional needs.

Sometimes, people appreciate an informal heads-up in advance of a more formal announcement, especially when it comes to bad news, such as changes in policy, budget cutbacks and so forth.

Talking about what bad news may lay ahead gives people an opportunity to talk among themselves, console each other and maybe even come up with solutions. Giving people advance warning of bad news allows them to express their concerns and realize they're not alone in their feelings.

30. How Do You Know When it's Time to Go?

Only you can determine if it's in everyone's best interest for you to step down from a volunteer position.

Under ideal circumstances volunteers will remain with an organization for years. Yet, unfortunately, there are instances when it's in everyone's best interest to move on.

Here are some clues to know if it's time to go:

- Your work as a volunteer continues to suffer.
- Your relationship with the volunteer manager is on the skids.
- Your position description doesn't match your strengths and/or interests.

Source: Laura Benjamin, President, Laura Benjamin International, Colorado Springs, CO. Phone (719) 266-8088. Email: info@LauraBenjamin.com

31. Three Rules for Delegating Effectively

When you're in charge...

These three delegation rules will help put you at ease when turning over jobs to colleague volunteers:

1. **Put it in writing.** Provide an outline of what is to be done that includes a description of expected outcomes.

2. **Confirm that the assigned project is fully understood.** Ask the volunteer to describe, in detail, what it is she/he will be doing from beginning to end.

3. **Ask for update reports.** Instruct the person completing the task to submit regular reports stating what's been accomplished to date.

32. Share Legitimate Concerns With Appropriate Staff

If you experience something during your volunteer time that just doesn't appear right — a procedure or someone's behavior, for example — don't let it slide or simply complain to a fellow volunteer. Take the concern directly to a paid staff person. Let them decide if or how the issue should be addressed.

As a volunteer, it's sometimes easy to let something pass and think "it's not my job to address those issues." But if employees are unaware of what's taking place, it's likely that the issue won't be addressed.

Unless it's a rare situation in which someone is always looking for faults they can complain about, employees are grateful to receive constructive input — both positive and negative — from their volunteers.

33. Stay Focused on the Big Picture

You've seen it happen. A volunteer gets so caught up in details of a project or issue she/he loses sight of the primary purpose or goal. And then there's the individual who gets off track of the overall goal because of wanting to see that her/his idea gets top priority.

Exemplary leadership

As a leader, do your part to stay focused on a project's primary purpose. Don't allow yourself to get sidetracked. And when you see others making petty issues the focus of attention, attempt to bring the group back to the primary task at hand. Here are two techniques for doing so:

1. Suggest that the group come back to the detail mentioned at the conclusion of the meeting — once the big issues have been fully addressed or planned.

2. Assign the suggested detail as a task to the person who brought it up and then get back to the larger issues at hand.

Distributing a printed meeting agenda in advance also helps participants to stay focused on what matters most and can serve as a tool to bring the conversation back on track.

34. Techniques to Make Your Special Event Stand Out

When galas, dinners, auctions and other fundraising events pack your community's calendar, competition for patrons and attendance can be a challenge. As a volunteer involved in various levels of special event planning, here are five ideas for you to help make your organization's event one people wouldn't dream of missing:

1. **Choose an off season.** The threat of inclement weather or chaos of the holiday season can make some dates appear undesirable at first. But take a closer look. Make the date work. Give people a reason to celebrate on a date they already anticipate — the Super Bowl, Academy Awards or Mardi Gras, for example.

2. **Educate your audience.** Consider an upscale luncheon or dinner seminar with a noted financial planner, author, motivational speaker, medical or legal figure who can offer guests general advice that can improve their lives.

3. **Borrow from popular culture.** Play up the reality show phenomenon. Host a "Survivor" dinner/treasure hunt (but with ample, well-prepared food). Bring the hands-on fun of "Extreme Makeover" by tackling a renovation project involving all those in attendance through donations or participation. Hold your own "American Idol" talent show with prizes for the winners and all participants.

4. **Gather celebrities.** Involve celebrities from the local news media, sports teams, business and industry, government and education. Pair up the media vs. city council members for a charity softball game. Have a "hidden talents" contest featuring the mayor playing harmonica, a popular meteorologist doing magic tricks and that big, burly college lineman reading poetry.

5. **Appeal to the family.** Make your event attractive to whole families and folks of all ages. When ticket prices are affordable, the setting pleasant and activities numerous and appealing to diverse crowds, people will follow. A pancake brunch combined with demonstrations by karate schools, high school choral groups, craft activities and a tour of your facilities can be a fulfilling family outing. Bring together as many diverse demonstrations, speakers, magic shows and performers as possible for a single event that can entertain a family for hours.

Talk About Keeping Your Cool...

The customer couldn't be pleased. First, he demanded the hostess turn up the air conditioning because he was too hot. Then he insisted she turn it down because he was cold. Too hot, too cold, on he went for his entire meal. Each time he demanded she adjust the AC setting, the hostess would nod, smile, walk back to the kitchen briefly, and return to her post.

When the high-maintenance customer finally left, another customer praised the hostess on how she handled the fussbudget. "You were so patient! You never got angry or upset. I am so impressed!"

"Oh, it was nothing — really," the hostess insisted. "We don't even have an air conditioner."

35. What Does it Take to be a Docent or Tour Guide?

Specialized volunteer positions

Thinking about becoming a docent or tour guide for your organization, but not sure if you have what it takes?

Here's what Yvonne Smith, volunteer coordinator, Milwaukee Public Museum, looks for in a docent/tour guide:

1. **A love of learning.** Initial training can take up to a year, plus you are always learning new material.

2. **A natural interest in something.** Ask to volunteer in an area you're interested in; that way you won't get bored learning new information about it.

3. **A willingness to work with people.** You'll be working with different types of groups, and you have to make the learning experience fun for them and be willing to answer questions.

Smith says tour guides and docents don't need a background in education. Many learn valuable questioning and management skills along the way. "It takes a lot of work to become a docent," she says, "but you get to expand on what you know and love in a beautiful, interesting setting."

Source: Yvonne Smith, Volunteer Coordinator, Milwaukee Public Museum, Milwaukee, WI. Phone (414) 278-2731. E-mail: smith@mpm.edu

36. Take Action to Avoid the 'Burnout' Syndrome

To remain enthused about volunteering, it's important for you to take steps to avoid burnout.

If you've been at the job for a lengthy period of time or contribute a healthy number of volunteer hours regularly, here are some steps you can take to help avoid burnout:

Change your routine. Even if there's a "best" way of doing something, it doesn't mean you can't alter the procedure now and then. Your state of mind, after all, is important, too.

Focus on teaching rather than doing. Show someone else how to do your job. Not only will it change your duties temporarily, it will also have you focusing on preparing someone who can now and then fill in for you or assume your duties when you move on to other assignments.

Celebrate both big and small achievements. Whenever you finish a task or a series of tasks, take a moment to relish those accomplishments. Give yourself a break as a reward. Take a walk. Those moments of self-satisfaction will also serve to motivate you for future assignments.

Set challenging but realistic goals. Short-term, quantifiable goals have a way of making any job more exciting. Whether it's setting a deadline or achieving a designated number of completed jobs, you'll find your work more rewarding when you're working toward one or more goals.

Blow Worries Away

When worries distract you from the task or joy at hand, here's a simple, childlike technique to brush them off. Imagine you're holding a bubble wand. Pretend to blow a bubble, filling it not just with breath, but with your worrisome thoughts as well. Now, with a gentle wave of your hand, send that distracting thought drifting away....

37.

SELF-IMPROVEMENT TECHNIQUE

Stop Negative Self-talk

Self-talk, we all do it. It's the small — but sometimes loud — voice you hear berating you when you lose out on a promotion, miss an appointment, misplace the car keys once again or say something you regret.

Although self-talk is normal, it can be very damaging to your self-esteem. Here are some ways to stop negative self-talk:

- **Just say no to negative words, thoughts and ideas.** When you catch yourself saying or thinking something negative, stop. Realize you're being negative and find something positive to do to distract yourself.

- **Acknowledge the feelings that are causing your negativity** (e.g., sadness, loneliness, disappointment in someone close to you, frustration, etc.), accept them and move forward.

- **Carry around a pocketful of paper clips.** Everytime you have a negative thought about yourself, hook the paper clips together in a chain. For each positive thought you have, remove a paper clip until you're paper clip-free.

- **When you look in the mirror, smile, don't frown.** Treat yourself the way you would a friend. Tell yourself how good you look in your new outfit; point out how nice your hair looks; learn to appreciate and focus on your good qualities.

Self-talk Exercise

Write down two columns of phrases: One on the left with the negative self-talk you've noticed and would like to neutralize, and a column on the right for its antidote or reverse self-talk statement. For example:

Negative Self-talk	Positive Self-talk
I'll never get it all done!	Look at everything I've gotten done so far.
I always screw things up.	I blew that one, but I also did (a positive thing).
I don't have enough time!	Everything that needs to be done will get done.
I wish I had (or hadn't) said…	It's OK to be human, to make mistakes. I'll learn from this.
Why does this always happen to me?	Just because it happened once, doesn't mean it will happen again.

Is it Your Turn To Mentor?

Has your life been touched by a mentor, someone who gave you the confidence and encouragement to aim high? Now it's your turn to give back. Is there a young volunteer in your organization with whom you can share your advice and insight? Reach out to that person and offer to be a mentor. Research shows that mentoring helps organizations by encouraging retention and promoting growth.

Responding to Criticism

Recognize that criticism is often based on the desire to be heard and recognized. Open a dialogue with your critic; pay sincere attention to his/her concerns; address those issues that can change and evolve; and explain your position on the issues that can't be modified.

Time Management Tip

Avoid being a perfectionist. With some jobs, it's actually more important to just do them — even if they're not done perfectly — rather than waiting "until you can give them the time they deserve."

Board Chairs Possess Great Potential

Whether you presently occupy the position of chairperson for your board or are considering it at some future date, it's important to recognize that the person in the chairperson's position has a tremendous opportunity to inspire all other board members. And whatever the board is inspired to do collectively influences an organization's entire constituency. You can raise your organization to an undreamed of level of accomplishment by first recognizing the potential of your position. Reach within yourself. Dream of what could be. Then begin to make it a reality and witness how others will follow.

38. Help Generate Needed Funds

Gift-giving ideas

Need to buy a gift for someone's birthday or other occasion? Look to the organization you serve as a volunteer! Chances are that agency has some item being sold as a way to raise funds — lapel pins, calendars, cookbooks, clothing, ornaments, etc.

By purchasing such items and giving them as gifts, you are accomplishing three objectives:

1. You are helping the agency raise money through your purchase.

2. You are making the recipients of your gifts aware of the fundraising project. (Maybe they will make purchases to give as gifts as well.)

3. You are providing friends or family with a very special and thoughtful gift.

39. Make the Most of Your Retail Connections

Ideas worth considering

Do you represent or have ties to retail establishments — restaurants, department stores, clothing establishments and more? If you do, consider how you might make those connections to benefit the organization(s) for which you volunteer.

Here are ways to use those retail ties to help a deserving organization:

✓ Seek permission for the store to publicize volunteer opportunities for your organization in advertising or in-store posters.

✓ Convince a retail establishment to sponsor an event or program.

✓ Get the store's employees to "give a day" of volunteering for a worthy project.

✓ Invite the business to host an open house for your organization at its location (during or after business hours).

✓ Ask for in-kind donations that the charity can use to reward or thank volunteers.

✓ Invite the retail establishment to donate a percentage of their weekly or monthly sales to the organization for which you volunteer.

✓ Seek permission to place donation boxes at each of the establishment's locations.

✓ Encourage the business to include a flyer about your organization (and volunteer opportunities) whenever it sends a mass mailing.

40. Come Prepared for Meetings

Meeting Time Saver

If your meetings are taking more time than they should, ask committees to provide reports in writing prior to your meeting. Consider sending them out to meeting attendees in advance along with your agenda.

All too often people come to meetings ill prepared. This in turn results in delays, diversions from the agenda and more, all contributing to what can be a frustrating experience for everyone in attendance. To set an example for others, here's what you should do to be thoroughly prepared for regularly scheduled meetings:

Review any materials that are distributed in advance. Prior to the meeting, read minutes, review the agenda and make written notes of key questions or issues you might want to address at the meeting.

Get important topics on the agenda. If there's an issue you want addressed, contact the appropriate person to get it on the agenda.

Arrive early. If materials are distributed when people arrive, you will have time to review them before the meeting gets underway.

41. Parliamentary Procedure Tips

Here are a few tips about parliamentary procedures you might not know about:

1. Calls of "Question" by members from their seats are not motions for the previous question and are simply informal expressions of individual members' desires to proceed to a vote; these calls are disorderly if made while another member is speaking or seeking recognition.

2. It is a general rule that no member should be present when any matter relating to him/herself is under consideration.

3. Abstentions do not count in tallying the vote; when members abstain, they are in effect only attending the meeting to aid in constituting a quorum.

42. Praise Publicly, Admonish Privately

When it comes to motivating fellow volunteers, remember — you can never acknowledge individual accomplishment in public too often. However, it's best to offer corrective advice in private.

Lead by example

43. Dream of Lofty Accomplishments

Whether you're a board member or volunteer for the organization you represent, make a point to dream of "what could be." Although it's a chief executive officer's job to lead strategic planning for a nonprofit, sometimes even CEOs need inspiration from others.

Here's one technique to help elevate your thinking: Imagine what could be accomplished if the organization — or even the volunteer department — were to receive a $1 million gift. How could it be used to advance the agency or institution? Would you build a new facility or expand your existing one? Would you map out a program plan that fulfills your organization's mission beyond its wildest dreams? Would you place the funds in a permanent endowment that would provide ongoing assistance for future generations of persons served by your agency?

As you dream about what could be accomplished five and 10 years down the road, share your thoughts with the CEO or other top management. Your dreams of what could be may provide the seeds that will one day take root in some great accomplishments for the organization.

Who says volunteers can't dream about "what could be?" Never underestimate what you can accomplish as a volunteer. Those dreams are just waiting to turn into reality!

44. Pay Attention to the Bottom Line

Although budget concerns may not be a part of your volunteer position description, you may be able to make a significant contribution to your organization by paying more attention to its bottom line. How so? By looking for solutions to these key questions:

1. How can I help the organization generate more revenue?
2. Where might this organization be able to cut back on expenses without hindering its services?
3. How can I help staff save time?

Any thoughtful ideas you can provide to these issues will most likely be welcomed by staff.

How might you help generate needed funds for this organization? What can you do to help cut expenses? Be alert to the ways in which you can help address budget issues as a volunteer.

45. Can You Help to Preserve History?

Do you have an interest in history? Then here's the perfect project for you!

Do you have a love of history? Perhaps you are skilled at researching or organizing files. Depending on your interests and talents, you may be able to perform a priceless service by helping the organization you are serving to research, compile and/or record its history.

Here are some examples of how you could get involved in preserving its history:

- Begin to assemble and organize artifacts from the organization's past — photographs, records, news clippings.

- Conduct interviews — recorded, videotaped or written — of persons still living who can provide insight into the organization's past.

- If you have a skill at writing, begin to write an historical account of the organization or some narrow aspect of it — the length and depth will depend on your degree of time and interest.

- Create an historical exhibit of some sort to be displayed in a high-traffic area.

46. Include Service Info in News Releases

Tout your volunteer relationships!

Whenever a news release goes out about you — professional achievements, career advancement, etc. — be sure to make note of your volunteer involvement. Not only does that reflect well on you, it also brings about positive visibility for the organization for which you volunteer. That information is a win-win for both you and your cause.

47. Does Your Salon Make the Cut?

Opportunities for specialty professions

If you own or are associated with a hair salon, you may have ample and unique ways to lend your services to a worthy cause. Perhaps some of these ideas will help you come up with a list of your own:

1. **Do a special promotion:** "Any clients who contribute two or more hours of service to [name of agency] will receive 20 percent off the cost of your next appointment."

2. **Enlist volunteers.** Have agency brochures (that list volunteer opportunities) on display in your wait area.

3. **Conduct a cut-and-style demonstration** as a program reward for a group of deserving volunteers.

4. **Make one of your agency's fundraising items** (e.g., cookbooks, lapel pins, calendars) available for sale to patrons who visit your salon.

5. **Convince your associates to give a portion of their day off as a volunteer** for the agency or volunteer as a group.

6. **Provide the agency with a number of discount coupons** that can be awarded as gifts to their volunteers.

Ever Question a Policy?

If you ever find yourself questioning an existing policy, don't act too quickly to get it changed. Instead, follow these steps:

1. Speak to the appropriate staff person and ask questions.
2. If you still see a problem, write down your concerns and possible solutions.
3. Share those concerns and potential solutions with the staff person.

48. Tips to Keep Your Cool During Emotionally Charged Meetings

Meetings can sometimes include emotionally-charged topics that need to be addressed by those present. And it's not uncommon for such meetings to degenerate into chaos and leave participants feeling angry and hurt. That's why it's important to go into such meetings psychologically prepared. If you can keep your cool and stay focused on the topic at hand, others will be more likely to follow suit, and your odds of reaching a logical solution will be more likely to succeed.

To help stay on track, go into your meeting with these principles in mind:

1. **Keep your cool.** Make a conscious effort to act and appear "pleasant" in spite of outside influences. Doing so will help you to maintain a higher level of comfort and concentration.

2. **Stay focused on the issue.** Don't allow personalities and the way in which messages are delivered color your thinking. Be mindful of possible solutions and compromises.

3. **Learn new mediation techniques.** Rather than disagreeing with a statement you consider to be inaccurate, first use the technique of repeating the statement back to the individual to allow him/her to hear what has just been said and perhaps alter or correct the statement: "So, Mary, if I heard you correctly, you believe we should turn away those in need of our services if we have reached full capacity. Is that correct?"

4. **Pick your fights.** It's better to speak up on what you consider a key point — and win — than to stand up to each and every statement with which you disagree. There's an old saying, "To use power is to lose power." Use your power sparingly and wisely.

5. **Try to be a calming influence.** Whether you think it's appropriate to add a bit of levity to an overly tense situation, or you find it helpful to step in and bring everyone back to the issue at hand, try to envision yourself as a calming but focused influence for those present.

6. **Reward positive behavior.** So often we tend to focus on the person who is exhibiting the negative behavior. If, instead, we would point out instances of positive behavior — so others present could take note — the mood of the meeting might turn more positive. Example: "Good thinking, Susan. I like the way you always stay focused on finding a solution."

Be psychologically prepared for meetings that may address controversial issues.

Dress for the Occasion

Whether or not your volunteer position calls for particular attire, it's important to dress appropriately for the occasion. Your presence on the job is a reflection of the organization for which you work. When others see you as a representative for the cause for which you work, in their minds, you are that organization. So whether or not a written dress code exists, be mindful of how you dress and appear whenever you're "on the job."

49. Marketing Idea for Those 'Selling' Items

Does your organization sell items as a way to raise funds: Christmas ornaments, holiday plants, calendars or items bearing your organization's logo?

If so, here's a marketing idea to try: Instead of simply selling the items, purchase whatever amount you can afford — as your own personal gift to the organization — then give them away to persons you feel could afford to purchase several of the items. Include a personal note with each gift: "I'm giving this to you because I know you will value it, but more importantly, because I'm hoping you will purchase several of these yourself with the intent of giving them to those who are important in your life."

With a free gift in hand, the recipient may be encouraged to purchase more of the items than he/she might have otherwise considered.

Do your part to help generate needed funds. Explore different possibilities for achieving your fundraising goal.

50.

Help Committee Members Gain Ownership

Help committee members create ownership of upcoming tasks by involving them in setting goals for the project at the first meeting. Then, put the goals on a large bulletin board in your meeting room or on a large piece of paper you can post at subsequent meetings.

New to the Job? Get Yourself Off To a Positive Start

Just getting acquainted as a new board member or volunteer? Rather than go an entire year without feeling totally "at home" in your new role, make it your responsibility to familiarize yourself with the organization and its services as quickly and as thoroughly as possible. To do that:

1. Make it a top priority to participate in all orientation and training procedures that are offered.
2. Ask for at least one thorough tour of the facilities.
3. Meet as many staff persons as is possible to learn something about what they do.
4. Ask for and review bylaws, volunteer job descriptions, policies, historical information and more.
5. Familiarize yourself with the agency's mission statement.

SPOTLIGHT ACCOMPLISHMENTS, SKILLS

How to Market Your Volunteer Experience to Prospective Employers

Volunteer experience can be an extremely valuable part of your resume. But in listing it, make sure to use relevant titles, skill headings and descriptions that match the job you want, says Regina Pontow, author of *Proven Resumes: Strategies That Increase Salaries,* and owner of provenresumes.com.

"While many job seekers gain excellent work experience as volunteers, stating 'volunteer,' or the name of the agencies where experience was gained, is often not impressive," says Pontow. In most instances, she says, job seekers can market their volunteer experience at a much higher level by labeling the skills they've developed.

Here's an example of how a person who volunteered for a university marketing association and as a coordinator for a nonprofit center serving meals to the homeless could better promote her skills when applying for a paid marketing position: Rather than using the heading "Volunteer Experience," and listing general information without citing numbers or specifics, the job seeker could list the volunteering history as so:

Volunteer Experience

Member — University of Utah Marketing Assn 1997-Present.

Volunteer — Hot Meals for the Homeless 1997-Present. Worked with students and academic staff to coordinate and manage annual association and marketing events.

The person could also use a heading that promotes how the volunteer experience applies to the job under consideration, and be specific about the scope of the projects completed:

Related Marketing / Program Management Experience

Program Management / Marketing Events Coordination, University of Utah 1997-Present

Project Management, Non-Profit Agency Experience 1997-Present.

Managed marketing events with up to 2,000 in attendance which required coordinating registration, topics and speakers with 12 committee members including the Marketing Association President and Dean of Business Administration program.

Source: Regina Pontow, Owner, Provenresumes.com, Bellevue, WA. Phone (425) 481-6088. E-mail: info@provenresumes.com Website: www.provenresumes.com

51. Strive to be a Person of Your Word

There's only one thing worse than someone who refuses to help or be involved: Someone who says he/she will help but then doesn't. If you agree to do something, stick by your commitment. You may decide you can't say "yes" again, but if you said it the first time, honor your pledge.

If you have said "you can count on me" to any of these or other requests, be true to the organization, those it serves and yourself by following through in a timely matter:

Dependability is key when it comes to volunteering. If you agree to do something, do it. No questions asked.

- Will you serve as chairperson?
- Can I count on you to make five calls?
- Will you be there to help?
- Can you serve a three-year term?
- Will you see that this gets delivered?
- Can you assist with orientation?
- Will you find three others to serve on this committee?
- Will you cover this part of our event?

52. Five Keys to Planning a Successful First-time Event

Planning an event from scratch? Answer these questions and you'll be well on your way toward its successful completion:

Take the lead in planning a new event for your organization.

1. What's the event's primary purpose? Any secondary goals? If so, what are they?

2. What resources will be required — financial, equipment/supplies, expertise and number of volunteers?

3. What three ingredients need to be present for this event to be a great success?

4. What key steps/actions need to take place between now and the scheduled event date (or project deadline)?

5. Who are the key people I need to enlist to make this event a successful reality?

53. Why Not Start a Volunteer Support Group?

Feeling stressed out? Need more support from fellow volunteers? You're probably not alone. Why not start a support group — just for volunteers?

Support groups can:

Volunteers helping volunteers

- Build a sense of community among volunteers.
- Enable volunteers to offer social and emotional support to one another.
- Allow volunteers to talk confidentially about how things are going for them.
- Provide an opportunity for volunteers to ask questions and get feedback.
- Enable volunteers to share ideas.

It doesn't have to be formal — just offer to meet once a month or so at a volunteer's home. The point is to offer a supportive setting in which to discuss questions or concerns that pertain to volunteering.

54. Three Tips for Managing Your Time

Time management for volunteers

To help you better manage limited volunteer time, follow these guides:

1. **One size does not fit all.** When it comes to multitasking, no single solution works for everyone. Pick the tactic that's best for you.

2. **Cut to the chase.** Avoid dwelling on an unfinished task. If there's a job to be done, just do it.

3. **Heading to a meeting?** Go unplugged. When you meet with someone, you're using a nonrenewable resource: your time. Don't let cell phone or pager interruptions waste it.

55. Willingly Give Committee's Report at Meetings

Don't rely on paid staff to give reports at volunteer meetings. Do your part to take ownership and assume that responsibility.

Too often, an employee gives a committee report at a board meeting rather than the chair of that particular committee doing so. It shouldn't be that way. If you are truly representing a particular committee or project, *you* should be the one to give the report. Your words carry more weight with fellow board members. Equally important, if you're the one delivering a report, you will find yourself taking greater ownership for what's happening.

If you find an employee has been giving the board report because "that's the way it's always been done," offer to assume the responsibility. Chances are the employee will be thrilled that you are asking to do it.

Make a point to meet with the employee prior to the full board meeting to discuss what to present. That way you'll both be on the same page should any questions or issues arise following your report. And if questions do come up, be sure the employee knows he/she can join you in providing detailed, accurate answers to the group.

56. Five Principles for Giving Knockout Facility Tours

If you ever give tours, here are five ways to become an even better tour guide.

Volunteers who give facility tours are generally "top drawer" assistants. After all, it takes a special individual who is capable of and willing to provide visitor tours.

Having said that, there's always room to refine our "tour giving" abilities even more. In the end, our objective should be to have a visitor walk away from a completed tour thinking, "Wow! That was an interesting and entertaining tour. I learned a lot about this place."

To make your tour even more polished, adopt these five principles:

1. **Know as much as possible about the organization for which you are providing tours.** The more you know about its history, its facilities and its programs, the larger your pool of information from which to draw.

2. **Recognize that, in the eyes of visitors, you *are* the organization you represent.** Dress the part. Be professional at all times.

3. **Prepare and practice diligently.** Depending on the level of training you receive, do several "walk throughs" with a friend as a way of practicing. Ask for feedback.

4. **Be sensitive to the interests of your visitors.** Welcome questions along the way and be prepared to spend more time at a stop along the way that may particularly interest your group.

5. **Be flexible and test new ideas from time to time.** Try sharing a new anecdote or stopping at a different location along the way, but stick to your schedule.

57. Plan a Mystery Dinner as a Fun Way to Uncover New Funds

Event type:	Murder mystery party		
Gross:	$13,000	Planning:	9 months
Cost:	$ 3,682	Attendees:	100
Net:	$ 9,318	Volunteers:	15
Revenue:	Ticket sales, raffle, auctions, sponsorships		

Here's a fun volunteer-driven fundraising event to consider organizing! Any actors among your group?

A 17th century manor home at a Louisville country club is the perfect setting for a murder mystery party hosted by VSA arts of Kentucky, a nonprofit that provides educational opportunities through the arts for children and adults with disabilities.

Guests arriving at the clubhouse enjoy food, drinks, a silent auction and musical entertainment. After an hour, guests are invited to investigate the crime scene. Local thespians act out an original script created by the board president and another member. Guests are then given sleuth's guides, an official accusation form and 30 minutes to solve the mystery.

While the results are being tabulated, guests can participate in a live auction featuring artwork created by children with disabilities. The person who solves the mystery in the shortest amount of time wins the grand prize, a soft sculpture created by an adult artist with disabilities.

VSA arts of Kentucky has partnered with Barnes and Noble to promote the event. The Louisville bookstore features a special murder mystery display and distributes bookmarks and bag stuffers publicizing the event.

Where to Go for Murder Mystery Kits —

Mystery Maniacs: www.host-a-murder.com
Mysteries on the Net: www.mysteries-on-the-net.com
Tailor Made Mysteries: www.tailormademysteries.com
Haley Productions' Interactive Challenges: www.haleyproductions.com

The murder mystery party has proven so popular that the organization has decided to host a similar event in Bowling Green. "Because most of our board members live in Louisville, we've decided to partner with a local theater group in Bowling Green," says Ginny Miller, executive director for VSA arts of Kentucky. "We'll use the same format, but they'll provide the facility, actors and other volunteers."

Tickets for the murder mystery party are $50 per person in advance or $35 per person for groups of 10 or more.

Source: Ginny Miller, Executive Director, VSA arts of Kentucky, Bowling Green, KY. Phone (270) 781-0872. E-mail: vsaky@bellsouth.net

58. Identify Your Personal Passion Points

What is it about this organization that truly energizes you? Do you know?

To keep yourself motivated as a volunteer or board member, it's important to recognize what makes you passionate about giving time and becoming more involved. Identify your passion points and you'll find your experience much more rewarding and most likely also find you're a more productive volunteer as well.

Keep yourself energized

To identify what most energizes you:

1. **Jot notes during or after a meeting or event.** List what you enjoyed most and why. You might also want to list what you disliked most and why.

2. **Review your notes a day or two later.** Then consider what activities should be your focus as you zero in on what will most motivate you.

59. Seize Opportunities to Tout Your Charity's Accomplishments

Be an ambassador for your cause.

People like siding with a winner. That's why you shouldn't hesitate to make mention of your organization's accomplishments whenever the opportunity presents itself — during a social gathering, among your friends and family, at your place of employment and elsewhere.

To make it easier to tout accomplishments:

1. **Keep a list of known achievements.** Whenever you learn of a new accomplishment made by the organization you represent as a board member or volunteer, write it down. Keep a list of noteworthy items to which you can refer.

2. **Seek out news worth bragging about.** Ask the organization's employees about what's been happening in their departments. Carefully read all communications put out by the organization, identifying accomplishments worth adding to your list.

3. **Talk to those who are served by your organization (e.g., students, patients, youth, etc.).** Ask for their perceptions. You will no doubt hear some testimonial gems that could be shared with others.

60. Make Every Minute of Your Volunteer Time Count

As a volunteer, you may occasionally find yourself with a few free minutes on your hands. Perhaps the group task went more quickly than planned, or the tour group didn't show because of bad weather or a scheduling conflict.

While you could sit back with a cup of coffee and the newspaper until your shift ends, you could also use this rare free time in more productive ways.

After all, it takes just 10 minutes to:

- **Offer an idea.** Submit an idea in the volunteer suggestion box. (Have no such box? With volunteer manager's OK, use free time to make one.)

- **Do a walk-through.** Walk through your agency to offer assistance to people who need escorting or directions, tidy up and share a warm smile with staff, clients and visitors.

- **Brew up a pot.** Make a pot of coffee for the next volunteer shift and/or clean up the volunteer break room.

- **Help other volunteers.** Check on other volunteers to see if they need a hand getting their tasks done by the end of their shift.

- **Keep everybody healthy.** Use an antibacterial wipe or spray to sanitize phones, countertops, keyboards and other work areas to help prevent spread of colds and flu.

- **Share thoughts in writing.** Handwrite a note of thanks, praise or support to a co-volunteer, staff member, client or supervisor, or draft a letter to the editor praising co-volunteers' efforts in a recent special event or other milestone.

- **Help staff.** Approach a staff member and say, "I have 10 minutes available; how can I help you today?"

Be Prepared
To Make Decisions

If you find yourself appointed or elected to a leadership position, don't straddle the fence when a decision is needed. Often times, no decision on your part is worse than making the wrong decision.

After seeking sufficient input from everyone involved, weigh the pros and cons, then make a choice and move forward. Procrastinating about what to do generates anxiety among group participants and eats away at their enthusiasm.

Don't second guess yourself. You were placed in that position to lead and you have it within you to do just that.

61. Combine Holiday Celebrations With Acts of Kindness

Turn your holiday get together into more than just a social event.

During the first week of December, BEAN (Seattle, WA) members, a networking group that are also volunteers, get together to celebrate the holidays at a local bar or restaurant. They enjoy appetizers, drink specials, socializing, but also use the event to help local nonprofits.

Every holiday celebration is coupled with a food, clothing or toy drive. Howard Wu, president, says members want to keep in the spirit of the season and do something extra besides volunteering. The event, one of the biggest turnouts of the year, spreads donations around to area nonprofits that can use the items.

The holiday drives help members recognize that giving doesn't have to stop when December is over. They also couple other clothing drives with events for summer and back-to-school times.

Source: Howard Wu, President, BEAN, Seattle, WA. Phone (501) 325-2372.
E-mail: Howardw@beanonline.org

62. Calendar Highlights Volunteers, Generates Funds

The Hutcheson Medical Center Auxiliary (Fort Oglethorpe, GA) has found a way to get their volunteers and community leaders into the homes and businesses of their community.

For the past year, the auxiliary has been working on their 2007 fundraising effort — an auxiliary calendar featuring medical center volunteers, physicians, the hospital CEO, a chief of police and a mayor. Funds raised will be donated to the medical center for patient related services.

"The idea was developed after a volunteer was given a calendar produced by a woman's century club and she thought it would be an exciting new fundraiser for us," says Teresa Nance, auxiliary manager.

Above is the February photo from the Hutcheson Medical Center Auxiliary's 2007 Calendar.

Nance says the auxiliary began creating the calendar in 2005. "The calendar was introduced to our entire auxiliary membership during a semi-annual business meeting and all were enlisted to sell 25 calendars."

The calendar features 13 color 9 X 12 inch photos, including a group photo of the 125-member auxiliary volunteers as the calendar's cover. Photos were taken at various spots in the community, including a local amusement park, high school and historical sites.

"The decision to feature the volunteers was simple," says Nance. "This calendar is our first and we wanted to highlight our wonderful volunteers. The volunteers are well-known in their communities and we felt the calendar would sell well highlighting the organization."

The auxiliary was able to cover the cost of producing the calendars ($6,159) by selling $7,000 in advertisements. Members are selling the 5,150 calendars for $10 each.

Source: Teresa Nance, Auxiliary Manager, Hutcheson Medical Center, Fort Oglethorpe, GA. Phone (706) 858-2832. E-mail: tnance@hutcheson.org

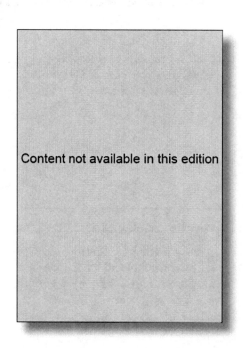

Content not available in this edition

63. Channel Nervousness Into Useful 'Delivery' Energy

Here are some tips for improving your presentation skills?

Does your throat tighten and your pulse race as you take the podium to present a formal speech? If so, you're not alone. The fear of public speaking is the No. 1 phobia among Americans, outranking even the fear of death.

So how do you stop your knees from knocking when you speak before an audience? Here are tips to transform your nervous energy into an effective delivery strategy:

Do —

✓ Use deep breathing exercises to calm yourself.
✓ Shake your hands to get the blood flowing. This makes your hand movements more natural.
✓ Visualize yourself giving your speech. Imagine yourself speaking with confidence in a loud, clear voice.
✓ Focus on your message. Ease tension by concentrating on your content and audience rather than yourself.
✓ Use the lectern/table for support if your legs start to feel weak.

Don't —

✓ Drink coffee, tea or other caffeinated beverages before the presentation. They'll make you more anxious.
✓ Forget to make a restroom stop prior to the speech.
✓ Hold full-sized notes. The audience can see them shake. Use 3-by-5-inch cards instead.
✓ Overuse gestures. Too much gesturing can make you appear even more nervous.
✓ Apologize for being nervous. You don't want to call attention to the problem. Remember nervousness does not show nearly as much as it feels.

Think About It

■ The most significant service is often the service that is unseen. Leadership versus servantship. They're equally important.

---

64. Learn From Other Organizations' Successes

Be willing to share the ideas and knowledge you have gained through past volunteer experiences.

If you have the good fortune of volunteering for a number of organizations, learn from what they are doing right and apply that knowledge to this organization. Perhaps orientation procedures are better organized at another nonprofit, or maybe one has a particular technique used to motivate its volunteers. Share whatever it is they are doing well with the staff of this organization. Here's how to do that:

1. Whenever you're attending a meeting or a function at another nonprofit and witness some method or idea that impresses you, write it down.

2. Then make a point to contact the appropriate staff person at this organization and share your observation. Explain why you think the idea or technique is worth trying.

Once you've done that, it's up to the staff to determine if your observation is worth duplicating. Either way, you've done your part.

On the Lighter Side....

A 10-year veteran volunteer receiving her retirement award: "Chaos, panic and disorder. Yes, I believe my work here is finally done."

---

65. Identify Colleagues Who Might Want to Volunteer

Could the organization for which you volunteer use even more volunteers? If so, you probably have several colleagues or contacts who might enjoy the opportunity of joining you.

Volunteers recruiting volunteers

To help surface individuals who you may not have considered as interested volunteers, analyze your many affiliations — your workplace, clubs or civic organizations, your place of worship, etc. Identify one or two people from each of your affiliations, then approach each — one-on-one or with a personal letter — asking them to give your organization a try.

Use a format similar to the example at the right to help identify your various affiliations and make your top picks.

CONTACTS WHO MIGHT WANT TO VOLUNTEER		
AFFILIATION	NAMES TO CONSIDER	NEXT STEP(S)
Workplace	Mark Wallace Sarah Feinstein	Contact at work Contact at work
Kiwanis	Harvey Mattern Tom Feld	Personal letter Personal letter
1st Presbyterian	Mary Ellen Engle Trish Hartfield	Phone Phone
Sheffield Alumni Board	Sam Dunwoody	Personal letter

66. Offer to Assist, Fill in for Fellow Volunteers

What if a fellow volunteer offered to help with a project you were heading up? Or what if another volunteer knew you had a full platter and suggested filling in for your assigned work slot to lighten your load? Wouldn't that be a pleasant surprise?

Remember The Golden Rule as you work with fellow volunteers.

As a leader, your proactive action in assisting other volunteers will not only be appreciated, but will also help establish a tone of cooperativeness among all volunteers. When they see someone else offer to assist without being asked, they will be more likely to do the same. Additionally, those you approached will hopefully want to return the favor at some point.

Surprise your volunteer colleagues. Offer to assist them. Your kindness will produce positive results.

67. Know How to Make Proper Introductions

Although you may have been taught the procedure for making proper introductions at some point in your life, here's a mini refresher:

Helpful protocol

• Present a junior person to a more senior person in a business setting, regardless of age. Mention the senior person's name first.

• When two people are of equal rank, introduce the younger person to the older person.

• If you're unsure of age differences or status differences, make your best guess. It's better to have an awkward introduction than to have no introduction at all.

New Year's Resolutions

Made your New Year's resolutions yet? It's never too soon (or too late) to decide on one or more. Here's a suggestion: At each meeting you attend this year, compliment someone on doing something well.

---

68. Share What Other Nonprofits are Doing

Be a source for great ideas...

You no doubt come in contact with other nonprofits. Perhaps you have attended another charity's fund raiser. You may receive mailings from other area agencies from time to time. Share that information with the cause for which you regularly volunteer. Who knows what those officials might learn from what others are doing?

Here are a few examples of how you might provide useful information to the organization for which you volunteer:

1. When you attend another nonprofit's function — a fundraising event, an open house, a program — share any printed materials and what you liked about the function with your charity.

2. Whenever you receive something in the mail from another agency — lists of annual contributors, newsletters, annual reports, etc. — pass it along to the appropriate person at your charity. The staff may find a useful idea after reviewing it.

3. If you have been approached by another organization to become involved in some capacity — to volunteer or to become a member or serve on a committee — share information about the approach that was used, and whether you found it effective.

69. Rewards for Teen Volunteers

Go for it! Whenever you help someone else, you become the winner. You forget about your own problems, and you become a happier person.

You're a teen. Your life is hectic with school and activities. But being a volunteer can benefit you in many ways.

Volunteering at a hospital is a great choice, especially if you're interested in the medical field.

You can hang out with your friends and even get letters of recommendation for college or a future job.

But more important are the personal rewards you'll receive. Where else can you interact with people of all ages, races and personality types? You can contribute to your community by being a volunteer and feel good about yourself.

Source: Grenda Pearlman, Director Volunteer Services, Saint John's Health Center, Santa Monica, CA. Phone (310) 829-8208.
Sharon Knox, Director Community Services, Emerson Hospital, Concord, MA. Phone (978) 287-3201.

70. Three Ways to Increase Your Personal Ticket Sales

Successful events

If you share responsibility for selling tickets for an upcoming event being held to benefit your organization, try to surpass your ticket sales goal by:

1. **Moving up your deadline.** If you are to sell 100 tickets in 30 days, move your deadline up by 15 days. Then, any tickets you sell after that time will be "extra."

2. **Getting others to sell for you.** In addition to those tickets you're trying to sell, convince a friend or family member to sell additional tickets on your behalf. You may double what you were able to do on your own.

3. **Publicizing that you have tickets available.** E-mail co-workers and friends. Bring tickets to public functions and announce that you have them for purchase.

71. Audience Participation Results in Sellout Event

Want to create a more memorable event? Let your guests in on the action!

Guest interaction makes the Diamond Ball, a fundraiser for the West Valley Arts Council (Litchfield Park, AZ), one of the most popular events of the season. In fact, the ball has sold out almost every year since its inception in 1994.

"We try to pick a theme that allows our guests to get involved," says Development Manager Judi Switanek.

The Diamond Ball featured a roaring '20s theme, complete with a speakeasy, Tommy guns and music from the Broadway musical and Academy Award-winning movie, "Chicago." Guests were encouraged to dress for the occasion, and many chose to don flapper dresses and zoot suits.

The structure of the event also lends itself to greater audience participation. "We try to keep talking to a minimum," says Switanek. "People come to have fun, not sit through a lengthy auction."

In accordance, the live auction is limited to about nine items. The auctioneer is also allowed to double- or even triple-sell certain items. That is, when bidding continues to escalate between two people, the auctioneer can offer to go down in price, but only if both parties agree to purchase the item up for bid. While you can't do this with every item, some things lend themselves nicely to it, says Switanek. It also creates a new level of excitement and keeps the auction moving.

The uniqueness of the Diamond Ball has made it quite popular — so much so that it typically sells out several months in advance. "We used to send out a 'save the date' card, reminding people about the ball, but due to its popularity we stopped doing that," she says. Now they send out the "Gemstone Gazette," a newsletter featuring articles about and photographs from the event, a few months after the ball. The back page focuses solely on next year's event and allows guests the opportunity to secure priority seating.

Source: Judi Switanek, Development Manager, West Valley Arts Council, Litchfield Park, AZ. Phone (623) 935-6384. E-mail: jswitanek@westvalleyarts.org

Volunteer-driven events

At a Glance —	
Event Type:	Black-tie
Gross:	$341,000
Costs:	$146,000
Net Income:	$195,000
Volunteers:	200
Planning:	8 months
Attendees:	600
Revenue Sources:	Ticket sales, sponsorships, auctions, raffle

72. Be Faithful About Meeting Follow-up

You've just finished up a meeting and everyone present — including you — was asked to complete a number of tasks before the next regularly scheduled meeting. Will each of your assignments be completed thoroughly and on time?

Appropriate follow-up is crucial after a meeting. If tasks aren't completed, there's no point in meeting.

To help pay greater attention to follow-up, and set an example for others, follow these guidelines:

- Remember to bring your calendar to each scheduled meeting as a reference tool.

- As a meeting is getting underway, make a "to do" heading in your notes. Then, as discussion takes place, write down any actions required of you following the meeting. Next to each item include an official deadline date or your own self-imposed deadline.

- Later that day or the following morning, review your notes to refresh your memory and make any additional notes in your calendar.

- Rewrite the tasks in your calendar daily until they have been completed as a way to keep them in the forefront.

To ensure everyone follows up on assigned tasks following a meeting, consider these suggestions.

Creative News Release Idea

Have you taken a business trip or attended a conference lately? What information did you bring back that will help your organization grow and prosper? Compare and contrast the way you do things with the way others you met do them.

73. Bring Your Children Into the Act

Family volunteering

If Your Job Is Media-connected

If you work for the media, take advantage of your position to gain greater visibility for the organization you're helping:

1. Head the public relations committee.
2. Help determine publicity strategies
3. Make public appearances on behalf of the agency.
4. Organize a press conference.
5. Train a staff person on news release preparation.
6. Help develop a standard press packet.
7. Oversee the production of a promotional video.
8. Help develop a list of feature story ideas.

Looking for a way to instill positive values in your children or set a good example for them? How about partnering with them on a volunteer project?

Jean Crocker-Lakness and her sons, Jimmy, 19, and Alex, 16, have been volunteering at Hamilton County Parks (Cincinnati, OH) for more than two years. Alex and his mother assist on winter hikes through the parks, and Jimmy volunteers once a month at the Sharon Woods gift shop.

"I enjoy doing it, because I believe in service and in giving back to the community," says Crocker-Lakness. "I want to share that with my children and impart my values on them."

Crocker-Lakness and her husband, Jim, have been volunteering for years. She's on the slate for president elect of the PTA, and he's active in their local church. They're both members of the Sierra Club and political activists. In fact, their sons have joined them on two anti-war marches over the past decade.

"It's part of our heritage," says Crocker-Lakness. "We're Quakers, and we believe in involving our children in our values."

A few years ago, the entire family went on a service trip to Colorado through the Sierra Club. They worked with the National Forest Service, pulling weeds and taking out fire circles. "It was a great experience, because other families went on the trip as well," says Crocker-Lakness. "The boys really enjoyed meeting kids from other parts of the country."

Because the boys were exposed to volunteering at an early age, they've learned to take the initiative on such projects. "We're so proud of them," she says. "In addition to learning about community service, they're also learning valuable skills such as operating a cash register and interacting with people."

Crocker-Lakness encourages other parents to volunteer with their children. "Don't be discouraged if it takes you a while to find your niche," she says. "Find something your kids are interested in. It's a great way to connect with them."

Source: Jean Crocker-Lakness, Volunteer, Hamilton County Parks, Cincinnati, OH. Phone (513) 891-9450. E-mail: crockejw@email.uc.edu

74. Learn to 'Operate on a Higher Plane'

Inspire yourself

Keep Meeting Attendees Alert

To keep everyone "on their toes" during your next meeting, explain that you will be sharing a "hidden answer" with the question given at the conclusion of the meeting. Those writing the correct answer to the question will receive a prize.

The fact that you volunteer already demonstrates your caring capacity. That's a given. But beyond that, each of us sometimes needs to work at conducting our daily lives on a higher plane — surpassing our normal capacity.

How one defines "operating on a higher plane" is different for each of us, based on our own unique set of circumstances. But the *way* in which it is defined is universal. Conducting our lives on a higher plane means "stretching" ourselves — our capacity to do good and to care and to set an example — beyond our limits. It's a regular examination of how we live our lives and then consciously striving to improve upon it.

Your power to choose allows you to conduct your life on an increasingly higher plane.

75. Volunteer Center, Nonprofit Groups Join Forces to Raise Money

In the true spirit of cooperation, 145 people participated in the second annual Human Race, a 10K run, 5K run/walk and 1-mile fun walk, planned and organized by the Volunteer Center of Southwest Michigan (Niles and Saint Joseph, MI).

"The Human Race is a unique opportunity for individuals, families and businesses to work together to raise funds for the nonprofit organization of their choice," says Sharon Peeters, business manager.

The event is held in June at the Fernwood Botanical Garden and Nature Preserve. The race/walk is open to anyone, regardless of age or ability.

Here's how it works: People register by completing a registration form and submitting an $18 event fee to the Volunteer Center. Participants then contact their favorite nonprofit organization to be sure it qualifies to participate in the Human Race. They use the contribution form to collect cash or checks from friends, family, neighbors and co-workers who sponsor them to participate. All checks are made out to the Human Race.

Participants may collect for more than one charity, but need to use a separate form for each.

All registered participants receive a race T-shirt, refreshments after the race and two-day admission to Fernwood. Prizes are awarded to the first-place male and female runners. The top three finishers in each age group (male and female) are recognized with a medal.

Fourteen organizations benefited from the Human Race, which raised almost $8,000. Participating groups receive 90% of the money collected. The remaining 10 percent is retained by the Volunteer Center. The Juvenile Diabetes Research Foundation raised the most money this year.

Source: Sharon Peeters, Business Manager, Volunteer Center of Southwest Michigan, Niles, MI. Phone (269) 683-5464.

Collaborative events — As you consider various types of events, don't overlook the possibility of partnering with another local nonprofit. By joining volunteer forces, you may be able to accomplish even more!

At a Glance —

Event Type:	10K Run, 5K Run, 1-Mile Fun Walk
Gross:	$13,000
Costs:	$5,000
Net Income:	$8,000
Volunteers:	30-40
Planning:	20 months
Attendees:	45 runners/walkers; 14 organizations
Revenue Sources:	Event fees, sponsorships, contributions

76. Proper Planning Pays Aplenty

The more you plan for success, the more likely you are to succeed in pursuing both personal and professional goals.

Here are some of the many benefits of proper planning:

Benefits of proper planning

- Planning gives you the opportunity to not only determine the exact results you want, but also identify what obstacles are in the way and how to overcome them.

- The more you plan, the more you drive the goals you want to accomplish into your subconscious mind where they take on a motivational power of their own.

- It's estimated that one planning minute saves at least five minutes in execution.

77. Recruit and Mentor Two Able-bodied Volunteers This Year

To really make a difference, make a personal commitment to recruit — and nurture — at least two new volunteers this year. Whether they are friends, business associates or family members, make a point to identify and approach only those individuals you think would make the best fit.

Set a personal goal to recruit other volunteers for this worthy cause!

Meet with your top choices, explain what volunteering for this organization entails, and point out that you're committed to helping them as they get familiar with the work of the organization.

Recruit and nurture two or more volunteers, and you'll unleash a tremendously positive force.

78. Do You Have an Aptitude for Art?

Make the most of your God-given talents.

Art, whether it's storytelling, poetry, music, dance, sculpture or painting, can have a soothing — even healing — effect on people. If you have an aptitude for creating beautiful works of art, why not share that talent with the people you serve?

Gracia Sears has been a volunteer chaplain at Crouse Hospital (Syracuse, NY) for more than four years and has gradually incorporated her talents as a painter into her chaplain role. "Art is a great addition to patients' stays here," says Director of Volunteers & Spiritual Care Nancy Stewart. "Gracia's paintings hang throughout our department."

Patients also have the opportunity to select one of her paintings to hang in their rooms. Another volunteer digitally records photographs of the paintings and organizes them in a catalog from which the patients can choose.

"Gracia also brings her easel and paints to the hospital, so the patients can watch her create," says Stewart. "She just keeps quietly expanding her role, and we've received wonderful feedback so far."

Source: Nancy Stewart, Director of Volunteer Services & Spiritual Care, Crouse Hospital, Syracuse, NY. Phone (315) 470-7046. E-mail: nancystewart@crouse.org

79. Tips for Keeping Annual Events Fresh

Are you involved in planning an annual event for your organization? Some events lose their pizazz over time. To keep the public enthused about your event, follow these steps.

As a volunteer, are you involved in planning and putting on an annual event? If so, here are ideas to bring to your next meeting to help keep the event exciting:

Rotate planning committee members. Set a term limit (one to three years) for volunteers to serve on the event planning committee or specific subcommittee. Bringing in new people will help generate fresh ideas. Likewise, if you've fulfilled a specific volunteer role for a number of years, look at the advantages of allowing someone else that opportunity and you fulfilling another task related to the event.

Include diverse groups. Ask teenagers, senior citizens and every age group to be involved in planning activities. Have the group meet several times to brainstorm, then agree on the most appealing ideas to include in the final program.

Write reviews of just-completed events. Have as many committee members, volunteers and attendees as possible anonymously complete post-event evaluations that include suggestions for how to improve it in the future, and parts they want to see repeated. Use the feedback to incorporate changes next time.

Avoid predictability. Even the Academy Awards and the Grammys would be dull if audiences knew in advance who would take home the Best Picture or Record of the Year statuettes. Throw in a few "wild cards" at every recognition dinner or other annual event, even if it means creating new categories or honors. Go all out to ensure the recipient will be pleasantly surprised and audience delighted.

Keep the best, toss the rest. Change is good, but take care not to eliminate surefire crowd pleasers in the process. If a favorite band keeps guests dancing and laughing until dawn, book it for the next year before the night is over. When the community raves about the corned beef and cabbage at your St. Patrick's Day fundraiser, keep the same caterer for every year. Determine what can easily be changed to keep things new, but not at the expense of longtime favorite draws.

Thanks, Giving Volunteers

This Thanksgiving season, particularly this Thanksgiving year, we are grateful for who you are and all you continue to give to worthy causes.

You're there in the early morning hours and during the quiet of night.

You're working hard even when you're out of others' sight.

You're stepping forward readily when no one else will budge.

You take on tasks so willingly and never bear a grudge.

We thank you for your loyalty, your enthusiastic style.

We recognize and appreciate how you go the extra mile.

— S. Cloyed

80. Get 'Influentials' Involved in Your Cause

Selective recruitment

Did you know that 10 percent of the American population tells the other 90 percent what to buy, whom to vote for and where to eat? They're called the "Influentials," and they're the subject of a book by Edward Keller and Jonathan Berry.

Influentials aren't necessarily the wealthiest or best-educated people, but they are actively engaged in their local communities and wield a huge amount of influence within those communities.

So how can the Influentials help the cause for which you volunteer? Because of their enormous power and influence, these individuals make excellent recruiters. If you can win over just one Influential, you may get nine other persons to follow, simply through word of mouth.

For more info, check out Keller and Berry's book, *The Influentials: One American in Ten Tells the Other Nine How to Vote, Where to Eat, and What to Buy* (www.simonsays.com).

81. How About a 'Best Friends' Campaign?

Volunteers recruiting volunteers

If the organization for which you volunteer could use more volunteers, members or both, here's a unique way to help accomplish that. Organize a "best friends" campaign among your fellow volunteers to reach out to new recruits.

Form a Best Friends Campaign Committee to develop a plan that encourages all volunteers to participate in this recruitment effort. Perhaps host an event to which all volunteers are encouraged to bring their best friend.

Whatever plan you develop, the idea of inviting your volunteers' best friends to consider volunteering (or becoming members) makes for a fun way of reaching out to new individuals.

82. Do What's Fun and/or Fulfilling

Volunteer for projects that you find energizing. Doing that will keep you coming back for more!

All too often, newly enlisted volunteers are understandably assigned jobs based on their professional background and experience. A teacher, for example, is assigned to work with children. An attorney is called on to assist with legal matters. A plumber is assigned to the buildings and grounds committee. The result may too often be: "I'm really not enjoying this. It's too much like what I do for a living."

There will be plenty of opportunities for you to offer your expertise on particular issues. However, before you are inadvertently assigned to a committee or project, don't be afraid to say you prefer to do something that has little to do with your profession. By speaking up, you may find the experience to be much more energizing, and you'll be a better volunteer because of it.

83. End Meetings on a Positive Note

When you're in charge...

While it's important to start meetings with a motivational message to get attendees fired up about being there, it's also important to give them something positive to take with them as they leave.

End each meeting with a positive message that is directly related to your organization or cause such as, "With your help we can achieve our goal of...." Or, end with a positive message from a motivational speaker or well-known world leader. Doing this reinforces those topics that were presented at the meeting while letting volunteers leave feeling good about having been a part of it.

84. If You Have a Talent for Writing...

Share your God-given talents.

Articulate writers are hard to come by. If you have an aptitude for writing, let the appropriate staff person know of your interest and willingness to do some writing that needs to get done.

Here are a few ways in which volunteer writers can contribute:

❑ Write articles and/or edit the agency's newsletter(s).

❑ Produce an occasional feature story that the organization can pitch to the news media.

❑ Take responsibility for producing timely news releases.

❑ Write or edit internal documents — volunteer handbook, orientation materials, etc.

❑ Write or edit marketing materials used by the agency — brochures, letters, etc.

❑ Prepare and/or edit grant proposals.

❑ Make a long-term commitment to write about the organization's founding and history.

❑ As a recognition tool, write monthly or quarterly profiles about other volunteers or board members that can be prominently displayed.

❑ Write public service announcements about the agency and its work.

85. Don't Let Differences of Opinion Sidetrack You From Your Goals

Keep your cool. Stay focused on what matters most.

If you truly believe in the cause for which you're working — and that's an important "if" — then it's imperative you not let differences with staff or other volunteers get in the way of your dedication to seeing the cause's mission fulfilled.

It's not uncommon to get emotionally sidetracked. There may be instances in which you feel an employee let you down or another volunteer is causing problems. Add to that something going wrong with an important project or program in which you were involved, and you can be sent into a tailspin. Suddenly your enthusiasm wanes, and you find yourself thinking it may be time to throw in the towel.

When instances such as that occur, take time to reflect: "Do I really want 'people' to end my relationship with a cause in which I believe so deeply?" Remember this fact: People will come and go, but this cause, and the need for its services, will continue long into the future.

So next time you find yourself having second thoughts about your connection to this cause, be sure to separate the people who happen to be present from the organization and its overall, positive mission in the community.

Calling Tree Tip

Prior to using the calling tree, instruct the last person(s) scheduled to be phoned to call the originator of the message immediately after receiving it. This lets the originator know the message made its way through the entire list, as well as how long it took to do so.

86. Look to Your Neighborhood for Help

If you're involved in a cause or a project in which your neighbors may have a vested interest, it might be worth your time to enlist their help.

Getting the job done

For example, are you tired of seeing your neighborhood park in shambles? Ask your neighbors to pitch in and help. Pick a Saturday morning and recruit volunteers to clean up the park. Have them bring shovels, rakes and garbage cans and clear the area of garbage, rocks and empty bottles. You may be surprised by their willingness to help.

87. Track Your Personal Recruitment Efforts

How much are you helping to recruit new volunteers or members for your organization? Doing so might be one of the best contributions you can make to assist the cause for which you volunteer.

If you are involved with recruiting volunteers or members, keep an up-to-date progress report of how you're doing. Why? Because it's a constant reminder of how much time you're putting into recruitment efforts, and monitoring your progress will also motivate you to do more.

Complete a monthly recruitment chart such as the example illustrated here. Try it for at least three months to see if it becomes a useful tool in your recruitment efforts.

MONTHLY RECRUITMENT CHART

Name _____ Date _____

	Contacts	Action Taken	Results	Follow-up
1.				
2.				
3.				
4.				
5.				
6.				
7.				
8.				
9.				
10.				

88. Board Members Have Fiduciary Responsibility

Fiduciary: "One, such as an agent of a principal or a company director, that stands in a special relation of trust, confidence, or responsibility in certain obligations to others."

Whenever one accepts the position of board member or board trustee of a nonprofit organization, a solemn commitment has been accepted to look out for the best interests of that agency throughout his/her term of office. Any personal or professional gain must be put aside. Every effort should be made to avoid even a hint of conflict of interest.

If you have the honor of serving as a board member of a nonprofit organization, recognize and fully accept your fiduciary responsibility to that organization.

Disagree With Finesse

If you take issue with something another volunteer or board member says, show some tact in the way you respond:

Wrong way — "I disagree. There's no way we should do that. It would be a poor decision."

Right way — "Although I can appreciate your suggestion, another alternative might be to.... Doing it this way would accomplish these goals...."

89. People Who Give, Live Longer

Benefits of volunteering

For older adults, it really is better to give than to receive, a University of Michigan (Ann Arbor, MI) study suggests.

The study, published in the journal *Psychological Science*, finds that older people who are helpful to others reduce their risk of dying by nearly 60 percent compared to those who provide neither practical help nor emotional support to relatives, neighbors or friends.

"Making a contribution to the lives of other people may help to extend our own lives," says the paper's lead author, Stephanie Brown, a psychologist at the university's Institute for Social Research.

For the study, funded in part by the National Institutes of Health, Brown analyzed data on 423 older couples who were first interviewed in 1987 and then followed for five years to see how they coped with the changes of later life.

In their first interview, couples were asked about any practical support they provided to friends, neighbors or relatives, including help with housework, child care, errands or transportation. They were also asked how much they could count on help from friends or family members if they needed it. Finally, they were asked about giving emotional support to or receiving it from their spouses.

Over the five-year period of the study, 134 people died. Brown found that people who reported providing no help to others were more than twice as likely to die as people who did give some help to others.

However, receiving help from others was not linked to a reduced risk of mortality.

"In other words, these findings suggest that it isn't what we *get* from relationships that makes contact with others so beneficial; it's what we *give*," says Brown.

Source: Stephanie L. Brown, Institute for Social Research, The University of Michigan, Ann Arbor, MI. E-mail: stebrown@isr.umich.edu

---

Protect Your Future Meeting Dates

If you deem it important to protect upcoming meeting dates for the year — scheduled board meetings, for instance — share those dates with those closest to you: Your family, supervisors and/or subordinates, etc. Doing so helps to further protect the dates.

---

90. Look for 'Donated Services' Opportunities

Look for opportunities that may benefit the organization for which you volunteer. Keep the organization in mind during your daily routine. You may be the catalyst who turns an idea into reality.

During your daily routine — outside of your volunteer time — be on the lookout for potential opportunities in which businesses might contribute their services to the cause you represent.

Look around. Be creative. You may discover a service that neither the organization nor potential donor realizes could be a great match. Ask yourself "who might donate what in the way of services?"

Need a few examples to get your wheels turning? Consider these:

- A laundromat owner who offers to clean a portion of an agency's laundry as an ongoing contribution.

- A corporation's advertising division that agrees to develop a nonprofit's publicity campaign and public service announcements.

- An auto dealer owner who agrees to service a nonprofit's vehicles on a cost-only basis.

- A printer who contributes the cost of producing an agency's annual report.

Learn to spot service opportunities that might result in a win-win for both the nonprofit and the business.

91. Be Ready for a 'Letter to the Editor'

If you have a way with the written word, look for appropriate opportunities to get the word out about the cause you represent by submitting a positive "letter to the editor" to your local paper.

Although not everyone reads these personal editorials, they do represent one avenue for reaching the public. Before submitting your letter to the editor, however, be sure to run it by the appropriate employee(s) to ensure your remarks are on target and so it comes as no surprise to the organization's top management.

Your letter will accomplish more goodwill if conveyed in a positive rather than negative tone. If pointing out something that you believe needs to be changed, be sure to also offer some realistic solutions.

Here are some editorial approaches you might take:

1. Citing a timely current event or community issue (e.g., teen pregnancy, adult illiteracy), tie it to the positive way(s) in which your organization is addressing this challenge.

2. Prior to a major event sponsored by the organization you represent, put forth a letter to the editor explaining why people should make a point to attend or participate.

3. Draft an editorial that lists the organization's accomplishments over the past year and stating why the public should take notice and support the organization's efforts.

If you have a talent for writing, your willingness to step forward and express an opinion — on behalf of the organization you represent — may be a highly beneficial contribution.

92. Cook-off Fundraiser With a Twist

Cook-off events are a great way to get your community involved in raising funds for your organization. Giving them a special twist — like the "Guys, Griddles and Grub" event hosted by Community Shares of Greater Cincinnati (Cincinnati, OH) — can make them stand out from the crowd.

"Guys, Griddles and Grub" features local amateur male chefs competing in six categories: appetizers, soup, salad, entrée, grill and dessert.

Jeniece Jones, executive director, says the fact that it is "guys only" grabs the public's attention. And, she says, the guys have a good time getting into some friendly competition with their fellow "chefs."

Primarily, the men — 40 to 50 per event — were found by placing notices with member organizations seeking men who enjoy cooking.

On the day of the event, each contestant brought their prepared dish. Attendees paid $35 to sample as many dishes as they liked, voting on their favorite dish. A winner was chosen from each category.

Along with the tasting, guests took part in a wine raffle and silent auction. Jones says the silent auction is a big draw because the items range from the unique, like expensive flat-weave rugs, to the universal, like restaurant gift certificates.

"Guys, Griddles and Grub" has grown in revenue every year. In 2007, the event raised 50 percent more than 2006, grossing $30,000 and netting $23,000. Jones says the contestants are not charged a participation fee because they cover their food expenses.

Source: Jeniece Jones, Executive Director, Community Shares of Greater Cincinnati, Cincinnati, OH. Phone (513) 475-0475. E-mail: jones@cintishares.org

Looking for a new fundraising event you and your colleagues can organize? Consider a cook-off.

At a Glance —

Event Type:	Cook-off competition
Gross:	$30,000
Costs:	$7,000
Net Income:	$23,000
Volunteers:	60
Planning:	8 months
Attendees:	250
Revenue Sources:	Ticket sales, silent auction, raffle, corporate sponsorships
Unique Feature:	Guys-only cook-off event

93. Be Prepared to Answer Questions About the Nonprofit You Serve

As an involved volunteer or board member, it's important for you to develop a solid understanding of the cause you are serving. Knowing answers to basic questions will not only help you be a more informed individual, but will also help in recruiting and involving others in your cause.

Take a few minutes to write down questions about your organization, then contact the appropriate staff person to get the answers.

To help illustrate the facts you might want to know, some basic questions are shown here.

Facts I should know about this organization —

1. When was the organization founded?
2. What is the mission statement for this organization?
3. What key programs/services does the organization provide?
4. How far do services extend geographically?
5. What is the current operations budget of the organization?
6. What is the annual payroll?
7. Does the organization have an endowment? What does it total?
8. How many persons are employed by the organization?
9. Who is primarily served by the organization? How many are served on an annual basis?
10. Does the organization have a long-term strategic plan? What are its key elements?
11. What have been the organization's major accomplishments during recent years?
12. What key challenges presently face the organization?
13. What are the primary sources of revenue (and percentages) for the organization?
14. How many volunteers are currently active on behalf of the organization?
15. What key statistics point out the need for this organization's services?
16. How does the work of this organization relate to current regional or national trends?
17. What percentage of the organization's annual budget comes from private gifts?

94. How to Avoid Talking Politics

Foster a positive volunteer climate of cooperativeness.

With local, state and national elections always around the corner, political talk tends to heat up. Avoid getting caught up in a political discussion that could hurt someone's feelings or saying something you'll regret by following these tips:

1. **Change the subject.** The simplest way to avoid getting into a political debate is to ignore the topic and replace it with another.

2. **Just say no.** If someone asks about your political views, simply say you're uncomfortable discussing such issues.

3. **Use humor.** Nothing eases tension like a joke. Think of a funny one-liner you can use to change the direction of the conversation.

4. **Answer a question with a question.** If someone asks who you're going to vote for, answer: "Who do you want me to vote for?" When he or she answers, reply: "I hear he is doing well in the polls."

5. **Make a quick exit.** If the discussion becomes too overwhelming, simply remove yourself from the situation.

95. Volunteer Builds Lasting Relationships With Patients

Amber Jenson has a full plate. She is married, works full-time managing an oral surgeon's office and attends school part-time for social work. Plus, she's volunteer of the year for the IHC Hospice (Salt Lake City, UT).

Amber Jenson

Jenson's sunny disposition, promptness and reliability all combined to help her win this distinction. "Amber has a way about her that makes persons feel good about themselves," says Volunteer Coordinator Kelly Kenyon. "She bonds with our patients in a way that is healthy and supportive."

This ability to bond with patients recently brightened one patient's life and taught Jenson a new skill. Once a week Jenson visits a quiet but fiercely independent woman who recently went blind. The woman was having a hard time coming to terms with needing help. Jenson would read and visit with her. "She's been through so many awesome things in her life," says Jenson.

When the woman would talk about owning a craft shop where she taught knitting and crocheting, "she just lit up," the volunteer says. "She told me how much she missed teaching." So Jenson asked for lessons. "She got so excited. Her head usually hangs, but when she talks about crocheting, she lifts her head up and smiles."

Lessons begin with the woman telling Jenson what supplies she needs. Then she tells Jenson what to do, demonstrates it herself and feels Jenson's work to check it. So far, Jenson has crocheted a large baby afghan and is learning to make baby booties.

By learning what passions drove her patient, Jenson made a lasting connection — one she tries to share with each patient she works with, says Kenyon.

"I get glowing reports from our RNs and staff members who pass along comments regarding Amber and the difference she has made in the patients' lives or even the family," says Kenyon. "One particular incident was when she continued to visit with a patient's widow to offer support. She was not instructed, but took the initiative to ensure the woman was doing well and that there were no complicated grief issues."

Sources: Kelly Kenyon, Volunteer Coordinator and Amber Jenson, Volunteer, IHC Hospice, Salt Lake City, UT. Phone (801) 887-6723. E-mail: Kelly.Kenyon@ihc.com

Whether you work behind the scene or on the front line, in one way or another, your contribution of time is helping the lives of others. Thank you for all you continue to do!

Content not available in this edition

96. Ways You Can Help Take Charge of the Suggestion Box

Does the organization for which you volunteer have a suggestion box? If so, offer to oversee it. If a suggestion box doesn't exist, offer to create and manage one. Here's what you could do:

Do your part to encourage volunteer input.

1. **Encourage others to make suggestions** (e.g., ways to enhance programs, cost-saving ideas, etc.), then collect and review them regularly with a staff person.

2. **Follow up on suggestions.** Contact the appropriate employee to discuss suggestions addressed to his/her department. Determine what can and cannot be done based on the suggestion.

3. **Thank those who make suggestions** (if not anonymous) and develop a system that rewards those whose suggestions get implemented.

97. Recognize What Matters Most in Your Life

Many who volunteer over a period of time come to realize that their gift of service is also a gift to themselves. For the more we give of ourselves, the more we are rewarded and fulfilled in our own lives. To give is to receive.

To achieve greater fulfillment in your everyday life, ask yourself these three questions:

1. What would I want to do if I had only a few months to live?

2. What would I want to have or do if I could have any one wish fulfilled instantly?

3. Would I be truly happy if I got whatever I thought I most deeply wanted? And what would I do with it?

After answering these questions, think about your work as a volunteer. Chances are, you'll find that the kindness you share with others is key to your ultimate happiness.

98. Be Prepared to Answer Visitors' Questions

Be alert to the ways in which you can assist visitors, even if that's not in your position description.

If you assist visitors as part of your volunteer duties, it's important to be able to answer their questions. To not be caught off guard by visitors' questions:

✓ Get together with other volunteers to review questions visitors have asked in the past. Write down each question and possible responses.

✓ Imagine yourself as a first-time visitor. What might you ask? Record these questions and answers, too.

✓ Each time a visitor asks you something that's *not* on your list, add it to the list so you will be better prepared next time it comes up.

Don't Overlook Involving Those Persons You Serve

Could you use more help with a particular volunteer-driven project? Don't overlook those you are serving — senior citizens, students, patients and others — as volunteer candidates.

Just because these people may be the recipients of your services doesn't mean they aren't capable of or interested in joining in the fun.

Sharpen Listening Skills

Know why we have two ears but only one mouth? To remember to listen twice as much as we talk! Employ these actions to better listen to visitors, other volunteers, staff and others:

1. Keep good eye contact with whoever is speaking.

2. Focus on the content of what is said rather than the delivery.

3. Allow the person speaking to completely finish his/her thought.

---

99. Not Leader Material? Followers Important, Too

Every volunteer, regardless of his/her position, is of equal importance. Never forget that.

If a volunteer leadership position isn't for you, help out those who choose to lead by being a good follower:

• Show up on time and stay until your shift ends or replacement shows.

• Complete assignments on time.

• Willingly volunteer to do more than you were asked to do.

• Treat your group's leader in a respectful way.

• Be a team player.

• Pay attention to details as you complete your assignment.

• Remember that good followers are just as important as great leaders!

100. Give New Assignments the '48-hour Test'

When someone asks you to serve another three-year term or take on the chairmanship of a new project, avoid giving an immediate response. Instead, ask questions about the duties and then say you'll get back with a response within 48 hours.

Be sure before agreeing to help.

Giving some thought to a request for help allows you to process whether you can give the job the attention it deserves. It's in both your best interest and that of the volunteer agency to be sure of your decision. Give thought to the time commitment required and whether your skills and interests match with the request. Can you perform the job with enthusiasm? Will work or family demands prevent you from following through as needed?

Two days isn't too long to give serious consideration to a serious commitment.

101. Wear Your Lapel Pin With Pride

If the organization for which you volunteer provides you with a lapel pin or has one available for purchase, wear it often and with pride. Doing so:

If you're fully committed to the organization for which you volunteer, you will find yourself acting as an ambassador on its behalf.

- Adds credibility to the organization because you're willing to promote it.

- Serves as a conversation opener about why others might want to get involved.

- Contributes to increasing the organization's visibility in the community.

- Demonstrates that the organization is important to you.

102. Have You Ever 'Journaled' Your Volunteer Experiences?

Maintaining a personal journal of volunteer activities can be beneficial, whether you're simply recording what you've done or including your feelings and observations.

Journaling can be a rewarding experience.

Journaling offers many benefits, among them:

1. Providing a lasting record of what tasks you completed and when.

2. Allowing you to reflect on your accomplishments as you write them down.

3. Enabling you to express feelings about a job that may be very emotionally charged.

4. Providing the opportunity to record ideas on ways tasks may be improved or completed more efficiently.

103. Key Fundraising Principles for Volunteers

To make your fundraising calls more gratifying and successful, follow these key principles:

Individuals willing to help in any aspect of fund development are a special blessing. And asking others for support can be a truly energizing experience!

1. Always opt for face-to-face calls rather than a phone call or letter.

2. Call to set an appointment rather than showing up unexpectedly.

3. Ask for the gift. At some point in the conversation, you need to step forward and make the ask.

4. Ask for a specific amount. Don't simply say "Would you like to contribute something?"

5. Be enthusiastic when making fundraising calls. Enthusiasm's contagious!

104. Be Alert to Assist the Hearing Impaired

Special needs volunteer colleagues

If your volunteer work involves assisting persons who have impaired hearing, here's what you can do to improve communications with them:

1. Get the attention of the person to whom you will speak before you start talking.

2. Face the hearing-impaired person directly when speaking. Or, if you know from which side the person hears best, talk to that side.

3. Reduce background noise or move to a quieter location.

4. During a sit-down meeting, seat the person where he/she can see each member present.

5. Ask the person what else you can do to improve communication (use pen and paper to write notes, if needed).

105. If You Have Access to the Wealthy

Ideas for Chapter Leaders

What can your chapters' leaders do to be more effective in their roles? Perhaps these ideas can provide them with some direction:

✓ Videotape a chapter get-together and show it at a later function.

✓ Produce and distribute a membership directory.

✓ Have a prize drawing for those who pay their dues on time.

✓ Develop a speakers' bureau of qualified chapter individuals.

✓ Create a chapter website with a link to your headquarters' site.

If your position in life allows you to connect with persons of wealth or with highly profitable businesses, use your connections to benefit the organization for which you volunteer.

Although you may find personal fulfillment and undoubtedly provide a valuable service as you volunteer to staff a reception desk, work in a gift shop or assist with programs or special events, your "connections" could also prove valuable to this organization you care about so deeply.

It takes just one significant gift to make a noticeable difference in what an organization is able to accomplish. Your willingness to make introductions and assist in cultivating relationships with the right people or businesses could result in a major charitable gift for this organization.

Serve as a key liaison with the financially capable by:

1. Never missing an opportunity to speak positively about the work of this deserving organization among others.

2. Being on the lookout for ways to involve persons of means with this agency.

3. Pointing out funding needs to those with financial capability.

4. Keeping staff informed of potential friend-building and funding opportunities among your circle of contacts.

5. Expressing your willingness to staff to assist with prospect identification, cultivation and solicitation to the degree you feel comfortable in doing so.

106. Under Promise and Over Deliver

Whenever you agree to take on an assignment, follow the old axiom: Under promise and over deliver:

• **Do more than is called for.** If you're expected to call three people, call six. If you've been asked to enlist five people, enlist 10 instead.

• **Beat the deadline.** Tell yourself to complete the project in less time than has been allotted for it.

• **Be a person of action.** If others are involved in the project, spur them on to complete their work on time. Look at the big picture and take on those tasks that are in need of someone's attention.

107. Eight Great Rules for Giving a Good Television Interview

When the local TV crews show up to spotlight your special event or volunteer project, do you run and hide?

Don't be camera shy! To be prepared to talk to the reporter about the good work you and other volunteers do, keep these eight tips in mind:

1. Look at the reporter, not the camera, when answering questions.

2. Don't be afraid to ask the reporter to repeat the question. This serves two purposes: It will help you clarify what the reporter is seeking, and it will give you time to think of a reply.

3. Talk to the reporter like you're having a conversation, the simpler the verbatim, the better.

4. Answer questions in short phrases. Think 15-second soundbite.

5. Speak in complete sentences. Work your organization's name into your answer. For example:

   > Reporter: *Why did you come out to your agency's cleanup day?*
   > Rather than replying: "Because I wanted to help and this is a good cause;" give an answer such as: "As a volunteer with [name of your organization], it's important that I give back to my community. And this annual cleanup day is a great way to do it. Plus, it gets me outside on this beautiful day!"

6. Do-overs are usually OK in a taped interview; ask for one if you need it.

7. If you don't know the answer to a question, say so. Reporters appreciate that over a made-up answer.

8. Remember to stand still when the camera is rolling, the more you move, the more you go out of frame.

There may be times when you're asked to represent the organization for which you volunteer: to publicize a new volunteer initiative, a special event or some other project. Here are some useful tips on how to conduct a television interview.

108. Help Others Find Reward in Their Work

As a board member or volunteer leader, it's important for you to recognize that your colleagues — who are also donating their time — should find some reward (and fun) in what they're doing. After all, that's why they're there.

You can play an instrumental role in helping paid staff see that other volunteers are enjoying their service experience.

1. **Look.** Be observant of other volunteers as they attend meetings and perform their duties. Is it obvious that they enjoy their work, or is it questionable?

2. **Listen.** When there's a question as to whether a volunteer may be uncomfortable or indifferent, ask an open-ended question or two and then listen carefully to his/her response.

3. **Assist.** If you discover a concern with a volunteer's level of fulfillment, do your part to help identify specific solution options. Ask yourself, "What can I do to help resolve this?" Depending on the seriousness of the problem, consider alerting the appropriate staff regarding your perceptions and possible solutions.

Be an example to your fellow board members or volunteers.

109. Got a Green Thumb? Share Your Garden's Bounty!

Don't forget to share your talents!

If you enjoy gardening in addition to your work as a volunteer, combine your passions in these and other ways:

✓ Bring cut flowers to your volunteer job. They brighten anyone's day.

✓ Help develop a landscape plan for the organization for which you volunteer.

✓ Give produce to employees, fellow volunteers and clients.

✓ Whip up a rhubarb cake, spinach salad or new potato salad to share.

✓ Plant and maintain flowers, shrubs, etc. outside of the organization.

✓ Conduct a gardening workshop for interested staff, volunteers and/or clients, if appropriate.

✓ Host a garden party at your home.

110. Advice for the Volunteer Phone Receptionist

Phone receptionist duties

Keep these protocol tips in mind if serving as receptionist:

• Tell the caller the reason for transferring the call before you do so. Then ask if it is all right to transfer their call.

• Call the department or person where you are transferring a call and make sure that they can take the call. If they are able to take the call, give them the person's name, their request, and any other relevant information.

• Then, return to your caller and give them the name of the person they are being transferred to, the department and the telephone number (if possible).

• When you're not sure to whom a call should be transferred, take their name and number and find out where the call needs to be directed. Also, give them your name and number as a reference in case the appropriate party does not contact them.

111. Volunteering Helps Diminish 'Bad Hair' Days

You Make God Smile

You may not know it, but you've lightened my load.

You may not know it, but you've brightened someone's life.

You may not know it, but your presence makes work more fun.

You may not know it, but you're an example for others to follow.

Did you happen to know you make God smile?

— S. Cloyed

The young executive was having one of *those* days. From a broken coffee pot to a traffic jam and office brush fires, she had no time for her priorities.

Then on her way home, she stopped by the local women's shelter where she serves on the board. She wanted to ask the shelter's director a question but found she wasn't there. An employee mentioned they were short on help and asked if the young executive could staff the phone for a few minutes. Reluctantly, she agreed — and ended up spending two hours fielding calls, providing encouraging words to callers and helping arrange for one woman to get a ride to the safety of the shelter.

As she drove home, she found she was relaxed. The tension of the day was gone. She felt good about herself and those two hours she had spent at the shelter.

The moral? Next time you're having a bad hair day, volunteer for an hour or two. It will reinvigorate you and get your priorities back in line.

Lightning Source UK Ltd.
Milton Keynes UK
UKOW01f0754060813

214894UK00007B/351/P